# The Educational Secret: Cultivating Entrepreneurial Spirit in Our Youth

*Ami Desai*

ISBN: 978-0-578-08778-8

## Dedication

To all the DVS Scholars, who, on a daily basis, taught me that anything is possible with relationships built on purpose, passion, and trust. Thank you for letting me be a part of your entrepreneurial journey to Greatness.

To all the educators who work tirelessly to make learning equitable, relevant, and engaging for students, and who strive to measure success beyond a test score.

## Thank You

To my parents who, at an early age, taught me about believing in the entrepreneurial spirit that was inside of me and for always supporting me in creating a life focused on following my dreams, giving back to others, and pursuing true happiness. I shall be forever grateful for the gifts you have given me.

To CM—for your unwavering guidance, encouragement, and vision…this would not have been possible without you.

And to RM—for your perspectives, critiques, and overall belief in my success…this has been a journey from independence to interdependence.

# Table of Contents

# There Is More to Life Than Just 'College and a Job'

Entrepreneurship and business practices are hardly taught within high school, within any school, but it is taught within these pages. In America, etiquette is pretty much left out to dry. Most students don't learn how to behave inside a conference room, let alone step inside one, or to use the proper utensils at a dinner table, or even know what business casual means. Recently I took a cruise and met a bunch of teenagers, all roughly 16, and none of them knew how to properly use a knife and fork to cut steak, except me. This shows a gap that displays a huge spectrum of etiquette understanding between children. While it was just a dinner course, that dinner course could represent the difference between landing an investor, and scaring them away with a sliding piece of steak. Kids and teenagers show traits of entrepreneurship early in their lives, such as jumping from idea to idea, being really excited about a thought or event, being hands-on learners, and always moving from place to place, and instead of recognizing these as assets, educators label these kids with disorders such as AD/HD. Negative labeling can damage a child's psyche and keep them from excelling as an entrepreneur and being successful and happy in life. Instead of discouraging with labels, why not encourage with teaching? In America, students need to be immersed in this exotic field of study. If students were allowed to freely express themselves in the studies that they are interested in, then we would see a huge increase in the number of entrepreneurs in the world.

It seems that while growing up, parents say, "behave yourself" or "sit right at the table" but with no indication of what it really means to behave or sit right. As a child, I grew up around my grandfather, who would always tell you what you were doing wrong, not to discourage, but rather to exemplify what to do right. He taught me how to present myself and how to act in front of adults. I have been graced with the knowledge of how to dress for a formal event, how to present myself to corporate managers, executives, etc., and how to behave at a dinner with management personnel. Without this knowledge, you make a bad first impression, and you can never make another first impression.

Unlike the norm in America, students don't learn how to create budgets, create an elevator pitch, speak in large crowds, or how to act in an office environment. Even just by watching the American version of the British TV show "The Office", anyone can learn how not to act/behave in an office setting. In a particular episode, the topic of public speaking is addressed, and the manager of the office tells his employee, "It doesn't matter what you say, it just matters that you're saying something that people care about!" While the principle of delivering a good speech is tucked inside the absurd comedy, children are still able to learn more about office ethics from sitting in front of a television screen for thirty minutes than sitting in school for eight hours.

I strongly believe that children should learn the importance of the actual business world. I believe that without these skills, it is difficult to get a job, maintain the job, and furthermore, be appropriate in a meeting. Entrepreneurship is essential because it promotes creative thinking, a mind set for problem solving, social skills, and business etiquette.

While attending a school based on entrepreneurship and being solely taught on how core subjects not only relate to the real world, I learned how to take advantage of opportunities, how to develop ideas with real world applications and, most importantly, how to be an entrepreneur. The school was strategically located near downtown Denver in order for scholars to be immersed in a business culture. Ami Desai was able to funnel out the noise, trim the fat, and get to the point of entrepreneurship and how to cultivate it without losing its essence. Having the experience of running a school that was focused on creating the young entrepreneurs of tomorrow gave Ami Desai the power to speak up against the major problem in education in America, and furthermore teaches how to cultivate the creative spirit of entrepreneurship.

**Emmanuel Ortiz**

**DPS Graduate 2012**

# Section 1: What Your Parents Never Learned

# Chapter 1: Cultivating Creativity Is Education

"Saying that more than 1 million students fail to graduate each year, Mr. Obama called on states to identify and focus on schools with graduation rates below 60 percent."

**- March 1, 2010, "Obama Addresses School-Dropout Crisis"**
**by Kara Rowland; *Washington Times***

"Many teenagers find lessons boring and irrelevant - and say the education system should be changed to suit their needs. Eight out of 10 said they were fed up with school and almost half said there were not enough courses to choose from, which limited their options in later life."

**- January 21, 2009, "School Is Boring and Irrelevant, Say**
**Teenagers" by Graeme Paton; The Telegraph**


Something happens to us as we get older. And it doesn't always feel good. We all experience it, but can't always explain it.

Things that seemed so much fun when we were 8 years old suddenly become silly. Those shows, songs, and games that put a smile on our face and brought us so much joy when we were one age, become the same things that others use to make fun of us or to make us feel ashamed.

I'm not speaking of the natural bumps along the road we travel to maturity, I'm speaking of those unexpected shocks that feel cruel, where we have to give up something – the way we feel, what we think, or something we like or prefer to do - not because we really want to but because someone else, with more power and experience than us, wants us to.

That's when we have to divide who we feel we are from what we are told is acceptable.

At our earliest age, it is most likely a parent, sibling, or someone close to our family who has this kind of authority or ability to pressure us. In a way, this is not so bad, because our ability to reason and make decisions on our own has not developed beyond a certain point.

But once we reach school age and our awareness and thinking gets better, there is something that continues to feel uncomfortable about the fact that the place where we are told we will learn the most about life and which will prepare us for the world seems to ignore and dismiss so much about our lives and our world. Although not true, it feels as if almost everything we care about 'doesn't fit' into education or school.

A friend of mine shared with me a first-person narrative of how he sees this dynamic playing out in the lives of students who feel disconnected from what goes on in their classrooms.

<<<<>>>>

"I just don't like school," Christopher told me, his head down, suddenly appearing to lose his appetite. My mere asking of how he was doing in school brought on a change in his mood that only a weatherman could describe. Excited and bright as he was - like sunshine - when the conversation centered around sports and entertainment like the latest music he listened to and the favorite sports he liked to play, Chris suddenly became gloomy, as if a storm cloud had taken over his heart when the subject shifted to school.

As his mentor and 'Big Brother' of over 2 years, I had gotten to know Chris pretty well, as well as his family, a younger sister and a mother who struggled to work two jobs to pay rent and bills. Out of concern for his worsening grades, his mom – Ms. Garcia – had asked me to not only talk to Chris, but also meet with his math and history teacher.

His math teacher, Mr. Dylan, a young man in his early 30's, outlined the test scores and progress reports that documented the decline he'd noticed in Chris's performance. And Ms. Hands, a woman of British descent in her mid-forties, gave me pretty much the same story, adding that Chris's behavior had become a distraction to other students and that he was coming late on an almost regular basis and not turning in homework, either.

Armed with these facts, I had taken my young friend to lunch this cold Saturday afternoon, not looking to scold or preach to him, but more so looking to understand what was going on in his life to explain this sudden change in his performance.

I took him to the Golden Dawn, my favorite diner, in my hometown, 30 minutes away from Chris's neighborhood – the first place we went to eat after we had been introduced to one another by a Big Brothers - Big Sisters program.

Over burgers, fries, and milkshakes, we began the meal only kicking around light subjects that I knew were more pleasant than a failed math exam – things like playing video games, which was his favorite hobby, and a little gossip about what he and his friends were sharing over the Internet.

We had never had a better time together – good food, telling jokes and stories, and 'people watching' – looking at couples, senior citizens, and families coming in and out of the diner and imagining together what their lives were like and what kinds of things they did for fun.

Thinking I had warmed him up for what I really wanted to get into, I decided to test the waters.

"So Chris, I spoke to Mr. Dylan and…"

"Ah man," he murmured as he rolled his eyes and put his head down, suddenly going into what looked like a mini-depression.

"No, I'm not upset with you or anything – you know you can tell me anything and I won't go crazy on you, or tell your mom without letting you know first. But, I'm concerned and just want to know what's happening in that class and also in History," I said trying to lighten the mood a bit.

"I just don't like school," he responded dismissively. "It's a waste of time. A lot of my classmates aren't graduating. They're already getting ready to drop out and take the GED so they can go and work."

"Is that what you want to do?" I asked, actually getting nervous, and preparing for the worst.

Chris sighed and staring off into space just said, "I don't know. But I'm definitely not into school like I used to be."

I was hardly surprised by what I was hearing. It just hit home because of how close I was to the person speaking the words. Although I had done pretty well in school, I didn't care for it too much either. But the reality that Chris was living in – from the Internet to pressures to experimenting with drug use - was far different than back in my days of high school.

We had our share of high school drop-outs back then but nothing like today.

It was six years earlier working as a political consultant on a political campaign when I first began to see how serious the drop-out problem had become. I could not believe the number of intelligent students who were *not* failing their classes but who had carefully decided to leave school, taking the GED instead, so they could begin earning money during the very same hours they would normally be in class.

What shocked me was how clear-thinking they were about their decision.

In most cases they weren't quitting school because they couldn't do the work that was required to pass. Rather, they were dropping out because they did not like school and felt it was not relevant to anything they felt passionately about.

*Why should I stay here if it doesn't help me do what I like, has rules that are strict, and keeps me from making money?* I imagined many of these teenagers saying to themselves, and, maybe more importantly, to one another.

The logic and common sense in their complaints regarding school and why they should leave were hard to argue with and I sympathized with many of them, especially those living in poverty and without much emotional support.

But while I agreed with much of what these students had pointed out about the shortcomings of school, there was something that kept me from accepting that their increasingly popular decision – dropping out – was the solution to the problem.

I noticed that in my conversation with Chris, and in previous ones, even though admitting he didn't like doing homework and that some of it was harder than he thought it would be, Chris never once told me that he did not feel he could learn, or that handling schoolwork was something he was incapable of.

I found the same to be true of most of the students living in the congressional district of the candidate I was working with – when we spoke to them, none said they were dropping out because they thought class work was something they just could not do. In fact, many of the students gave the impression that they were actually smarter than their teachers thought they were and that the work they were being assigned to do was not challenging.

I realized from these conversations with young people that their problem was one of motivation. They did not have enough of an incentive – in their own minds – to justify going to school as opposed to going to work.

Work generated money, which allowed them to buy things now. School was a place you had to go because adults said so. No comparison.

Early on in my life I knew there was a big difference between learning and school. And that the difference between learning and school was motivation, relevance, and interest. Students could learn anything that could be taught if they felt it was relevant to their lives. And students could be motivated to try and learn something, if they saw it had a relationship to something they had an interest in.

There were two experiences from my childhood that made me think that the motivation, relevance, and interest one can easily find in elementary school is missing from high school education.

The first was a memory of my art class in 1st grade. The teacher told us to draw a picture of anything that we liked. I drew a picture of my favorite football player – L.C. Greenwood of the Pittsburgh Steelers, who was famous for playing in yellow and gold-colored shoes. So, of course, I drew a picture of him in a pair of oversized yellow shoes and took it home to show my father, whose favorite team was the Pittsburgh Steelers. While watching the Steelers play the Los Angeles Rams in Super Bowl XIV, I kept the picture close by. In some way I felt closer to my Dad, connected to the game, with a sense of accomplishment and pride in myself.

Through this simple art class assignment, a teacher had allowed me the freedom to create something relevant to a current event (the Super

Bowl), and which interested myself and my family. School was a place where learning was fun and directly related to my world, however small it may be, compared to adults. I see this same process at work when cartoons are used to teach very young children lessons about life. There may be few other things in the life of a pre-schooler that bring together motivation, relevance, and interest like watching their favorite cartoon. But beyond the baby-sitting function these cartoons serve, they are also a form of learning, *outside of a classroom.*

The other experience that stands out to me is the statement my parents would make, and which I would hear other adults making to classmates of mine while we were in high school, which was, "*If you knew your school lessons like you knew those rap songs you would be doing better in school.*"

My friends and I would get so tired of hearing this and we always thought this was a strange thing for an adult to say because it was obvious to us young people *why* we were learning the lyrics to songs better than we were learning in the classroom – the words to the songs had great music behind them, were catchy, and it was cool to know them. With school this was not the case.

These examples showed me that creativity was a form of learning, and by the time I and most every other person reached high school, the sense of personal connection I felt when in 1st grade art class, and in learning my favorite song, was no longer present in a classroom, if it had ever been there.

That connection was gone, and with it a lot of personal motivation, sense of relevance, and interest in my studies.

Sir Ken Robinson says that creativity is as important as literacy – learning how to read and write. And I agree. He also argues that early on in the school experience of children they are not afraid to make mistakes and freely experiment and take chances and risks – not frightened of being wrong. But once they get older in their educational experience and become adults, he adds, the fear of making mistakes and being wrong takes over. He says we are educating people not into but *out* of their creative capacities. I also agree.

Percentage of 8th to 10th grade dropouts who reported that various reasons for dropping out of school applied to them.

| Reason | Total | Male | Female |
|---|---|---|---|
| **School Related:** | | | |
| Did not like school | 51.2 | 57.8 | 44.2 |
| Could not get along with teachers | 35.0 | 51.6 | 17.2 |
| Could not get along with students | 20.1 | 18.3 | 21.9 |
| Was suspended too often | 16.1 | 19.2 | 12.7 |
| Did not feel safe at school | 12.1 | 11.5 | 12.8 |
| Was expelled | 13.4 | 17.6 | 8.9 |
| Felt I didn't belong | 23.2 | 31.5 | 14.4 |
| Could not keep up with school work | 31.3 | 37.6 | 24.7 |
| Was failing school | 39.9 | 46.2 | 33.1 |
| Changed school, didn't like new one | 13.2 | 10.8 | 15.8 |
| **Job Related:** | | | |
| Couldn't work and go to school at same time | 14.1 | 20.0 | 7.8 |
| Had to get a job | 15.3 | 14.7 | 16.0 |
| Found a job | 15.3 | 18.6 | |
| **Family Related:** | | | |
| Had to support family | 9.2 | 4.8 | 14.0 |
| Wanted to have family | 6.2 | 4.2 | 8.4 |
| Was pregnant | 31.0 | | 31.0 |
| Became pregnant | 13.6 | 5.1 | 22.6 |
| Got married | 13.1 | 3.4 | 23.6 |
| Had to care for family member | 8.3 | 4.6 | 12.2 |
| **Other:** | | | |
| Wanted to travel | 2.1 | 2.5 | 1.7 |
| Friends dropped out | 14.1 | 16.8 | 11.3 |

DATA SOURCE: U.S. Department of Education, National Center for Education Statistics, National Education Longitudinal Study of 1988 (NELS:88) First Followup Study, 1990.

When I shared my thoughts with Chris, he told me, "Yeah, my teachers never tell us how learning any of this stuff matters! And school doesn't relate to anything I like doing. It doesn't tie together."

His appetite returning, he said to me, putting more ketchup on his uneaten fries, "That's all I want, the stuff they want us to learn to mean something and relate to what I'm into and what I want to do.

Right now I only do homework because I have to, not 'cause I want to," he said with an honesty I could feel.

"Well, Chris," I began, finishing my milkshake, "What do you want to do when you get out of school?"

Chris, half-smiled and looked almost embarrassed, a bit shy about answering.

"Alright, all that stuff I've been telling you about being a doctor one day is only to make my mom happy," he said, laughing.

"I never believed it either." I admitted, which made both of us laugh so loudly, the people sitting next to us in the diner began to stare.

Lowering his voice Chris said to me, "Alright I'll tell you because I trust you. If I could do anything, it would be one day owning my own football team."

"Really?" I said, somewhat surprised.

"Now, tell me how to get Mr. Dylan to teach me that!" Chris said, not realizing he had challenged me, his full attention on his plate, confident that what he was describing was impossible.

But as I thought over it silently I wasn't so sure.

Maybe a an 11<sup>th</sup> grade pre-calculus teacher could help a 16-year old get ready to own a billion dollar business.

# Chapter 2: You Can Learn Economics and Business Right Now!

"High school graduates will be making economic choices all their lives, as breadwinners and consumers, as citizens and voters. A wide range of people will bombard them with economic information and misinformation for their entire lives. They will need some capacity for critical judgment.

- James Tobin, "Economic Literacy Isn't Marginal Investment," *Wall Street Journal*, 9 July 1986.

"Mr. Dylan, the reason I'm calling you is to tell you that I had a chance to talk to Chris earlier today like I told you I would," I said over my cell phone.

"Great. I hope it will do him some good because I feel like I'm losing him and he is starting to fall behind at the most important time of the year for the class," Mr. Dylan said, his voice sounding as if he had been occupied before I called.

"Yeah, me too," I added. "Something came up during our conversation that I wanted to share with you."

"Sure, I'm listening," Mr. Dylan said, sounding as if I had his full attention.

"Chris told me something about himself I never knew before," I paused to make sure Mr. Dylan was paying attention. "He wants to own a professional sports team."

"Really?" Mr. Dylan said, sounding just like me when I first heard the news.

"Yeah, and he said something in passing, in reference to you that I want to take up as a challenge because I think it will help him."

"Wow, I'm all ears," Mr. Dylan said.

"Ok, Chris is a big fan of videogames as you know," I said.

"Right, so are a lot of his classmates. They talk about the games all the time. I don't understand any of them," he responded with a chuckle.

I continued, "But I noticed something about one of the sports games – *Madden Football*. I've played it myself and even a couple of times with Chris. Most people skip over it, Mr. Dylan, but at the beginning of the game you are given several options on how you want to play the game. One of those options is the 'Franchise' feature, which allows you to take the place of an owner or general manager making the business decisions of an entire sports organization. You get to see everything a team has to deal with from parking fees, player salaries, contracts from TV stations, and ticket prices." I shared.

"I did not know that," Mr. Dylan said, sounding very interested.

"Well, I know that nowadays most high schools don't teach economics or business. In fact, when I was in high school 20 years ago, I only had a small economics class that lasted for four weeks," I confessed from my experience.

"But, one of the parts of the Franchise feature shows all of the income and expenses of the teams you play with. And while I know high school students are taught how to read balance sheets, it is very clear to me that math is relevant to running a sports team," I explained.

"Definitely, without math you can't do any calculations that accountants and team managers would need to do to figure out how much money was going in and going out," Mr. Dylan said.

"Exactly! And that is all I want to help Chris see – that math and what you are teaching are relevant to what he wants to do later in life, especially owning a sports team. Would you be willing to just talk to him about this and show him how all of the math courses he has taken up to 11th grade can help him accomplish his goals?" I requested.

"It would be my pleasure. I'm a sports fan too!" Mr. Dylan concluded and we both laughed.

<<<<>>>>

Having more fun in taking on Chris's challenge than I expected, I called his mother to update her and asked if she would not mind if, for his birthday, which was the following week, I purchased the new edition of Madden for him – *Madden 2011*. She agreed, more I think, because of the point it would allow me to make to him than because it was a nice gift. If she hadn't known of my plan, she probably would have only seen it as another distraction keeping her son from doing his homework.

The next week, right after school, I stopped by the house and gave Chris a card and the gift, which he was overjoyed to receive, and then I asked him if we could play the game right then and there.

Pleasantly surprised, he put the game in, and I directed him into the Franchise mode.

"Why don't you ever go to the 'Owner's Box' section of the game?" I asked innocently.

"I don't know, my friends and I just like playing the normal games," He answered.

"But you want to be an owner of a sports team one day right, Chris?"

"Yeah, definitely," he responded starting to wonder what was up with my questions and sudden interest in a video game.

"OK, well then this is the part of the game you should care about, even more than the passing, running, and tackling action."

By now my young friend had sunk back into the couch he was sitting on, listening carefully to what I was saying.

"Chris, this game has every aspect of what you are looking for to learn what it would be like to be an owner. You have to consider advertising, ticket prices, the salaries of players, hiring coaches, how much to charge fans who come to the game."

"Yeah, I never thought of it like that after all of these years of playing," Chris said.

"I know, but take a look at this," I said as I pressed a few buttons on the controllers to show him how the income and expenses were listed for each team. "And guess what you have to know to be a great general manager or owner of a football team," I asked.

"What?" Chris said, already knowing I was setting him up for the answer I wanted to hear, or give.

"Math!" I said, laughing.

"You got me good man," he said.

"Football is a business Chris, and math is necessary to running every business. *Can you imagine not knowing math and having to sign paychecks each week and negotiate deals with the best players?*"

"No, you would be out of business real quick," he said with a knowing tone. "I see what you mean," Chris nodded his head while looking at me.

Knowing that I had made my point and wanting to give Chris a chance to think about it on his own for a while, I got up and began to head to the door, in the process catching Chris's mom around the hall in the kitchen leaning so she could listen to what we were discussing.

"Look, Chris, I went ahead and spoke to Mr. Dylan about all of this, and he said that he's willing to go over how relevant your math classes are to your interest in sports. I want you to go see him after class and talk to him."

As I got to the door I turned and said, with a big smile, "Oh yeah, happy birthday and enjoy your new game."

<<<<>>>>

This account relating to 'Chris,' and 'Mr. Dylan' - given to me by a friend who has been concerned about the dropout rate in American schools - captures much of what students, teachers, and principals deal with on a regular basis and offers a new perspective on how to help students become engaged again in their class work.

In the case of Chris, finding a connection between a video game and a class may hold the key to making his studies relevant to his goals and aspirations; for other students it may be a hobby, a language, a talent, or a family tradition.

But, because so much of the pressure that students face in regard to doing well in school is associated with their economic future – getting a job and earning money - perhaps the most important connections to be made can be found in helping students see themselves and what they aspire to do creatively in the relationship between class work and the workplace.

Since business and economics are such an important part of all of our lives and decisions regarding it affect everyone in one way or another, the fact that these two subjects aren't taught in elementary school and at the high school level is interesting, if not strange.

If nothing else, the most recent economic recession demonstrated that the lack of financial literacy, or knowledge about money and investments, played some part in what happened. People lost homes, jobs, and savings in large part because they did not understand economics, finance, and business, all of which can be taught at some level before college.

There are many ways to introduce economics into the classroom but one of the best and easiest is to show exactly what money is by teaching the relationship between the different currencies used by the world's nations. Students who are children of members of the United States Armed Forces – Army, Navy, Air Force and Marines – who live outside of the United States of America receive this kind of education in Department of Defense schools and get familiar with international economics at a young age because they have to frequently exchange dollars for the currency of the nation they live in to buy things and go places.

A friend of mine who grew up overseas as an 'Army Brat' on military bases in the 1980s knew the exchange rate between the U.S. dollar, British pound, German mark, French franc, Italian lira, and Spanish peseta every single day and would keep track of them with his older brother – even making up a game between them 'betting' on the value of the currencies each morning. This helped bring their world history class to life and improved their understanding of current events.

Also, since so many students in the United States are children of immigrants or are immigrants themselves from nations in Central and

South America, Asia, Africa, and Europe, focusing on the currencies of the nations they come from is an important way to help them feel more comfortable and educate their classmates about their heritage and background.

By bringing in different forms of money from all over the world and discussing their history in class – math, history, social studies, humanities, and art all come together – becoming more relevant and interesting to students and giving them a motivation to study harder.

Here is an example of what can be taught and discussed about different forms of money from around the world:

## West African CFA franc

Countries: Benin, Burkina Faso, Cote d'Ivoire, Guinea-Bissau, Mali, Niger, Senegal, Togo
Exchange rate (June 2011): 1 US Dollar = CFA 450.1798

- First introduced to the French colonies in West Africa in 1945. It replaced the French West African franc.

## Japanese yen

Country: Japan
Exchange rate (June 2011): 1 US Dollar = 80 yen

- Officially adopted in 1871 by the Meiji government.
- Third most traded currency in the world – after the euro and dollar.

### Euro

Country: Used by 17 of 27 nations in the European Union

Exchange rate:  1 US Dollar (June 2011) = .6855 euro

- Established in 1992 by the Maastricht Treaty.
- Used daily by over 300 million Europeans.

### Egyptian pound

Country: Egypt

Exchange rate: 1 US Dollar  (June 2011)= 5.936 Egyptian pounds

- First Introduced in 1834.
- All Egyptian banknotes are bilingual, with Arabic and English writing.

### Indian rupee

Country: India

Exchange rate: 1 US Dollar (June 2011) = 44.722 Indian rupee

- Believed to be first introduced in between the 16th and 15th centuries.
- India was one of the earliest places in the world to issue coins-around the 6th century BC.

Whether through using sports video games or foreign currencies, there are many ways to keep creativity in education and produce a learning environment where students are free to be themselves and even make mistakes in a classroom.  By constantly challenging classroom work to focus on creativity, motivation, relevance, and interest in relation to students, as well as test scores, homework, and quizzes; class and learning can come together in ways that hold the student accountable not only to parents, guardians, and teachers, but also themselves and one another.

# Chapter 3: The University of Self:
## 'School' Begins With Getting To Know Who You Are

"For the most part, children are natural, prolific, and happy daydreamers, and the process plays an important role in their developing lives. Too often, however, parents and teachers are quick to label daydreaming as a symptom of an Attention Deficit Disorder or the sign of a slacker in the making. A new study finds that "positive-constructive" daydreaming, even when heavy in pattern, is not related to psychological disorders as some have previously thought, but rather is a normal activity that reflects the daydreamer's imaginative tendencies and enjoyment of daydreaming.

There's actually a substantial amount of research connecting daydreaming in children with creativity, healthy social adjustment, and good school performance. A recent New Zealand study has found that imaginary friends benefit children's language skills and may also boost their performance at school."

**- "How Daydreaming Helps Children Process Information and Explore Ideas"; by Amy Fries; *Psychology Today***

"Know Thy Self"

**- Guiding principle of Socrates**

Could it be that some of the personality qualities that some believe make for 'bad students,' are also the traits of great entrepreneurs?

For years we have heard of how 'daydreaming', strong-headedness', and 'rebelliousness' interfere with the learning process and have to be 'corrected' or eliminated if a student is to achieve high academic performance and succeed in the world after high school.

But is that really the case? Is it possible that in trying to correct certain attitudes and behaviors in young people, we may actually be preventing them from succeeding at the highest level in life?

In an interesting commentary featured on the Public Broadcasting Services (PBS) Nightly Business Report program, Shonika Proctor, author of *Teen Entrepreneur Success Secrets* stated:

When I mentor teens I see their purpose, power, and determination as they put business ideas together. This experience has made me realize that entrepreneurship is not a course or class but a level of consciousness that many teens have but are unaware of. When given encouragement and opportunity they see their strengths and how they can be a teen entrepreneur, now. In experimenting and trying to figure out how to create their own identity, teens instinctively use the personality traits shared by successful entrepreneurs. They are creative, opinionated, and intent to challenge authority. They do not segregate work, learning, and play, which through the eyes of a parent can be misinterpreted as unfocused. Teens who are seen as unmanageable by their parents or teachers are often the ones displaying signs of innovation, fearlessness and leadership. If you are seeing these personality traits in the teens in your life, maybe it is time you reassess your perception of their potential. I've worked with teens that fit this profile who have overcome life challenges and negative labels to beat the odds in school, life and business. They have written and published books. They have designed and manufactured products. They have even been featured on national television. So I leave you with this thought: take your teens' aspirations seriously. Although they may not conform to the world around them, perhaps this is exactly the trait that will allow them to create their own world – a world we call a business.

Medical-Dictionary.com defines attention deficit disorder as "A syndrome, usually diagnosed in childhood, characterized by a persistent pattern of impulsiveness, a short attention span, and sometimes hyperactivity, and interfering especially with academic, occupational, and social performance."

But is this really the case? Do these characteristics really interfere with occupational and social performance?

David Giwerc, in an article, "The AD/HD Entrepreneur: Most Entrepreneurs Have It – It's Just A Matter Of Degree", wrote:

The United States is in the midst of an entrepreneurial renaissance. People are literally waking up to the idea that they can work for themselves and make a lot of money doing it. And, while there are as many types of entrepreneurs as there are businesses, most entrepreneurs share some common traits. They tend to be visionaries. People who go into business for themselves tend to be risk takers.

After almost a decade of coaching entrepreneurs, it has also been my observation that a majority of all entrepreneurs have Attention Deficit Hyperactivity Disorder, or AD/HD. They may not be taking medication and many of them haven't even been diagnosed, but anyone who knows AD/HD would recognize the signs. The chart below compares AD/HD with Entrepreneurship. As they use to say on those old TV shows, only the names have been changed. Once you understand what AD/HD looks like, you could easily conclude that virtually all successful entrepreneurs have AD/HD. Experts on AD/HD believe that Benjamin Franklin had AD/HD. Coincidentally, Franklin is also thought to be the first American entrepreneur. There is evidence that Thomas Edison had AD/HD, as did Henry Ford, Walt Disney and both of the Wright Brothers. You don't have to go as far back as Edison and Ford to find examples of successful AD/HD entrepreneurs. David Neeleman, CEO of JetBlue, has publicly acknowledged his AD/HD. Neeleman has chosen not to take medication for AD/HD and has instead learned how to use his "unique brain wiring" to his advantage, now that he better understands it.

Thomas Apple, the inventor/designer of the NASDAQ video billboard in New York's Times Square and a successful businessman, told ADDitude magazine how his undiagnosed AD/HD had affected his life: "I was 40 years old when I realized I really was a smart person," he says. Like many entrepreneurs and others who don't color in the lines, Apple had trouble as a child. "I was well on the way to delinquent behavior by third-grade," Apple recalls. "I thought, 'If I'm going to be treated this way, I might as well act this way.'" After his son and daughter were diagnosed with AD/HD, Apple took a hard look at his pattern of career difficulties and two failed marriages and realized that he probably had it too. A doctor confirmed the diagnosis. Apple now takes medication to treat his AD/HD, but he realizes that there's more to it than taking medication. ADD isn't a 'take two pills and call me in the morning' type of diagnosis," he says. "It is something that you have to do 24/7."

Apple's story about realizing he had AD/HD after first seeing it in his children is very common among adults who have been diagnosed. AD/HD is a genetic disorder. If a child has it, there is up to a 70% chance that at least one of the parents has it too.

| Signs of AD/HD | Characteristics of an Entrepreneur |
|---|---|
| Distracted, seems to always have something new to think about | Constantly has new ideas for how to improve the business |
| Starts several projects at the same time, may not complete any of them | Flexible. Approaches problems from several different angles, always ready to change direction if that is what is needed |
| Distorted sense of time. For example, will spend hours playing a video game without realizing how much time has passed. | Immerses him or herself in the job and often does not realize how much time has passed |
| Visual thinkers | Visionaries who paint a picture for others |
| Hands-on learners | Hands-on managers |
| Hyperactive | Always on the go |

In addition to the very real possibility that traits considered bad for school may in fact be positive factors in entrepreneurship and business, there is the reality that some of the exercises that help us become more familiar with ourselves are not taught in school, and even may be considered closer to AD/HD signs.

For example, 'daydreaming', visualizing or creatively imagining persons, events, and circumstances, can help us get more familiar with our own personality and interests, and even where we want to go in life.

Also, we can identify what we love to do the most by analyzing the activities we enjoy so much that we lose track of time when involved with them. Yet, one of the signs of attention deficit disorder is a distorted sense of time, where things like playing video games for extended periods of time are judged uncritically as negative activities.

Furthermore, one of the major qualities that most people agree is essential for success later in life is the development of willpower and the ability to persevere through difficulties, adversity, and challenges and the confidence that only comes after we have accomplished something we did not think we could do.

While school can give us academic instruction that is necessary – reading, writing, problem-solving, and knowledge of math and science and important group and social experiences – it struggles in the just as important area of giving us the kind of self-awareness and self-knowledge that can help us identify meaning and purpose in our talents, skills and interests and how to apply them in the world.

One of the most important lessons in life young people need to learn is how to 'reconceptualize' a negative experience into an empowering form of information. It is a skill that will help bring balance, discipline and optimism into their lives. And it is a common quality among entrepreneurs and great achievers in life.

When a shock, loss, or great emotional pain is suffered, great achievers have to build will-power and persevere through the turmoil. But this can only occur after they have found or given purpose to the experience. When purpose, meaning, or a valuable lesson that gives guidance is identified and accepted, an amazing form of energy is released in a person.

These concepts and processes are seen clearly in the work of Viktor E. Frankyl, a psychiatrist, advocate of logotherapy and a Holocaust survivor.

From two separate writings of Mr. Frankyl we connect these three vital principles – purpose, meaning and lessons. How they relate to both young students and entrepreneurs is what we hope to stress. From his book, *The Will to Meaning*, Mr. Frankyl writes (we place boldface on those points where we think agreement with our model most visibly exists):

**Ever more patients complain of a feeling of emptiness and meaninglessness**, which seems to me to derive from two facts. Unlike an animal, man is not told by instincts what he must do. And unlike man in former times, he is no longer told by traditions what he should do. Often he does not even know what he basically wishes to do. Instead, either he wishes to do what other people do (conformism), or he does what other people wish him to do.

I hope that I shall be successful in conveying to the reader my conviction that, despite the crumbling traditions, life holds a meaning for each and every individual, and even more, it retains this meaning literally to his last breath. And the psychiatrist can show his patient that life never ceases to have a meaning. To be sure, he cannot show his patient *what* the meaning is, but he may well show him that there is a meaning, and that life retains it: that it remains meaningful, under any conditions. As logotherapy teaches, **even the tragic and negative aspects of life, such as unavoidable suffering, can be turned into a human achievement by the attitude which he adopts toward his predicament.** In contrast to most of the existential schools of thought, logotherapy is in no way pessimistic, but it is realistic in that it faces the tragic triad of human existence: pain, death, and guilt. Logotherapy may be justly called optimistic, because it **shows the patient how to transform despair into triumph.**

And then, from Mr. Frankyl's *Man's Search for Meaning*, we read of the process of reconceptualization and the role of attitude in more detail –

specifically, in how it was a factor in the survival of Holocaust prisoners:

As we said before, **any attempt to restore a man's inner strength in the camp had first to succeed in showing him some future goal.** Nietzsche's words, "He who has a why to live for can bear almost any how," could be the guiding motto for all psychotherapeutic and psychogenic efforts regarding prisoners. **Whenever there was an opportunity for it, one had to give them a *why* – an aim – for their lives, in order to strengthen them to bear the terrible *how* of their existence**. Woe to him who saw no more sense in his life, no aim, no purpose, and therefore no point in carrying on. He was soon lost. The typical reply with such a man reacted to all encouraging arguments was, "I have nothing more to expect from life anymore." What sort of answer can one give to that?

**What was really needed was a fundamental change in our attitude toward life**. We had to learn ourselves and, furthermore, we had to teach the despairing men that it did not matter what we expected from life, but rather what life expected from us. We needed to stop asking about the meaning of life, and instead to think of ourselves as those who were being questioned by life – daily and hourly. Our answer must consist, not in talk and meditation, but in right action and right conduct. **Life ultimately means taking responsibility to find the right answer to its problems and to fulfill tasks which it constantly sets for each individual.**

Every entrepreneur – if they are to succeed – must accept that it is this attitude expressed by Mr. Frankyl that is the only one that makes no excuses for failure, seeing life as a path to define one's self, solve problems, and find answers to difficult questions. Every young person struggles with how to handle disappointments, frustrations, and temporary setbacks.

Reconceptualizing these experiences – giving them meaning and purpose – is a key to maturity and success.

<<<<>>>>

Perhaps the most difficult area in terms of following the guiding principle of Greek philosopher Socrates - 'Know Thy Self' - is in the area of cultural diversity in the classroom and how feelings of alienation are very real in the experience of some students of different racial backgrounds.

The gap in communication and connection is very real between students and teachers, in some cases, at times because of how racial background and cultural heritage can influence different views of history, current events, and interpretations of the classroom and school experience.

One of the clearest expressions of this gap from a student's point of view was published in the October 14, 2008 edition of the *Education news Colorado eNewsletter* (ednewscolorado.org).

In an article entitled, 'School Reformers: If You Want to Help, Listen to Youth,' a then-Freshmen Lorenzo Sanchez wrote:

I am now a freshman in college. As I look back, out of about twelve people who I hung out with in high school, only three graduated. This doesn't shock me, nor should it shock anyone who is familiar with the statistics regarding Latinos.

I think that it is fair to say that we spent most of the academic part of our high school careers in frustration. For me, it was for a different reason than it was for my peers. I was frustrated because of the lack of academic rigor. I knew that I was not being challenged nor was I being prepared for college. I wrote fewer than ten papers in my four years of high school.

Now, within my first month of college, I have written five papers. In high school I did not need to develop any study skills, so I didn't. I was tested over how well I could regurgitate what the teacher had said. I was able to pass the tests by simply showing up for the review the day before the test. Then after each test, I could forget what I had "learned" because I knew that it wasn't going to come up again. That doesn't work in college. I didn't do any homework either. One, it was rarely assigned, and, two, it was not necessary to pass. Homework wasn't essential; it was more like "busy work."

The worst part was that I knew that I was being robbed of an education; I knew that I was being put at a disadvantage while it was happening. I tried to do something about it, but I was trying to fight decades of systemic failure. I saw what was happening around me and felt like a one-man army.

The adults and students were concerned with passing and getting into college, not necessarily preparing for college. I don't know why this part was overlooked. I brought this to the attention of my teachers and administrators but for some reason they refused to acknowledge that this was an issue. They went so far as to consider me negative and unconstructive. Why couldn't I focus on the positive, the fact that everybody was passing? But just because we were passing didn't mean that we were receiving an education. The few of us who did make it through our public schools were just being set up for failure in college.

Unfortunately by this point, our public schools had already done an injustice to the black, brown, Native American, and Alaskan and Hawaiian native communities, and to the nation. I do place a lot of blame on our schools. The way I see it, if only one brown student in a school full of brown students was to drop out, then it probably had more to do with that particular individual. But if over fifty percent of black, brown, Native Americans, and Alaskan and Hawaiian natives drop out year after year, decade after decade, across the country, then there is something seriously wrong with our education system.

I know that a lot of people are aware of this crisis. I have seen teachers and administrators put their heads together to try and better serve this population of students. But how are middle class white people going to know how to educate *me*, *us*? They don't know what *I* need, what *we* need. They don't know what we have to go through every day.

In addition to our everyday personal struggles, we have to combat racism, sexism, discrimination and marginalization, and some of these we experience through our education. Even if they are aware, they don't know what to do about it. Yet despite the obvious culture gap, there they go, trying to find a solution. The people involved in our education, including teachers, administrators, policy makers, should be able to genuinely connect with the students.

Why don't they ever bother to ask *us*, the very people they are trying to serve? Why did they never ask any of my homies what they needed in order to succeed in school? Why didn't anyone ever ask us *why* we ditched class? Why didn't anyone ever ask us *why* we were disruptive in class?

Instead, the white adults immediately try to "discipline" us. We get removed from a classroom when we are "disruptive" or "defiant." In other words, we get removed from the classroom when we are annoying to the teacher, rather than for any serious violation of school policy.

How is removing us from the classroom and then "disciplining" us helping us learn? It only puts us further behind. I think that adults often assume the worst. Had they have bothered to sit and have a genuine conversation with any of my homies, they would have realized that all of us wanted to graduate and go to college, but we didn't have the right support. The majority of them were behind academically and nothing was happening to catch them up. How frustrated would you be if you were in tenth grade but you read at a seventh grade level, and the people who were being paid to make sure that you were receiving an education just tried to "discipline" you?

Why didn't they just ask us? Why didn't they seek our opinions? Why didn't anyone take us seriously? I have spent thirteen years in public schools full of low-income students of color. Is it fair to say that I have experience too? I probably have more experience inside the classrooms of public schools with low-income students of color than a lot of teachers, administrators, and policy makers.

The lack of change is discouraging. I have begun to think that maybe our education system hasn't been broken for over 50 years. Maybe, it's doing exactly what it's supposed to do.

While Lorenzo's writing may be difficult for some to accept, ignoring the central points he makes would be a mistake. What is clear in his words are two powerful opinions: 1) students feeling their own experience is not a part of, or respected by the educational process 2) alienation between students of one racial or cultural background and teachers that come from another.

These dynamics were part of what motivated a Pennsylvania school to experiment with classroom settings which separated students by race.

The explosive concept was too much for many in the media to resist not sensationalizing.

In a January 28, 2011 article published at AOLnews.com, 'Pa. School Defends Separating Blacks for Homeroom', authored by Dana Chivvis, we read, "A Lancaster, Pa., high school is under fire for implementing a new program that has created separate homerooms for black juniors."

But while the superficial focus pertained to racial identity, a far more intriguing element emerged in the story:

"In December, McCaskey East High School assigned its 275 11th-graders to 19 homerooms led by teacher-mentors. The black students were separated by gender and placed in three homerooms led by black teachers. The other students were similarly assigned to teachers with whom they'd had a prior relationship. All students were allowed to choose a different mentor or to opt out of the program altogether.

'We saw the need for mentoring of all our students,' McCaskey East Principal Bill Jimenez told AOL News.

…'The intent of mentoring at McCaskey High School is to build strong teacher and student relations, not separate students by race,' the Lancaster School District said in a statement. 'The high school is disappointed by the negative perception and focus on single racial composition programming.'"

*Mentorship and appreciation for culture, <u>not</u> racial segregation or separation* is what stands out in this story, it seems.

Could it be that a vehicle – in this case the presence of teacher-mentors – that would enable students to connect their upbringing and everyday experiences outside of school with their class instruction is what's missing? Would this in any way address Lorenzo's blunt concerns?

What is forgotten it seems, is that a young person first learns who they are and some form of culture *before* they enter into formal education. If a student does not see themselves in their classroom instruction or, even worse, if they are asked to negate or deny who they are and what they have learned about themselves and a culture in order to be accepted as a 'good student,' then elementary and high school becomes not just an irrelevant, uninteresting place where a student is unmotivated to learn, it can become perceived as a hostile environment.

Teachers who therefore can speak the language of students – engaging their personal experience and not asking them to negate who they feel they are – without compromising instruction, are in perhaps the best position to reach students that would otherwise be considered 'lost'.

The educational secret may therefore lie in the three areas touched on in this chapter:

Through the lens of entrepreneurship, the 'reconceptualization' of negative experiences and respect for the cultural self-concept, a young person may hold the key to an educational experience filled with motivation, interest, and relevance.

But maybe there is no secret at all when one understands that the word *education* derives from the verb *educe*, which means "to draw forth from within".

# Section 2: Individual Empowerment & Socialization

# Chapter 4: Building Your Personal Power Base

"Power consists in one's capacity to link his will with the purpose of others, to lead by reason and a gift of cooperation."
   - **Woodrow Wilson (1856 - 1924)**, *letter to Mary A. Hulbert, September 21, 1913*

"Knowledge is power."
      - **Sir Francis Bacon (1561 - 1626)**, *Religious Meditations, Of Heresies*, 1597

As an educator who has seen school systems from the inside out – the lesson plans, behavioral issues, administration, and financial realities – I have been struck by how the most important institution in the life of young people is too often a place that does not prepare them for some of the most important moments in their lives.

Helping students navigate the process of building their personal power and applying it in social interaction is not a common course in high school when it should be, and very easily could be. That this subject is not even available at the major college or university level of instruction is perhaps even more revealing and troubling.

Why is it that high levels of self-awareness, networking and professional and business etiquette are not taught publicly in our educational system when it is so important and even *expected* to be part of the makeup of an individual by the time they are in their early 20s?

Rather than trying to answer that question or wait for someone else to do it, I have decided to share lessons in these important areas with the school-age young people in my life, for whom I often serve as mentor.

To me, it is obvious that if a person – of any age – does not think enough of themselves or appreciate enough of the great qualities in their personality and know enough about their own talents, skills and interests, they are not prepared to tackle the world that not only awaits them, but which *confronts and challenges* them on a daily basis.

Again, we return to the important distinction I make between school and learning and how the difference sometimes revolves around how relevant and interesting the education is and how motivated a person is to receive it.

In every instance that I can recall, I have never interacted with a young student who was not interested in learning how they could become a more powerful person and successfully interact with others to accomplish their heart's desire. Once a person's most passionate ambitions are connected to learning, motivation seems to never be hard to muster.

It all starts with showing that individual their own personal power and how to access it.

In a comfortable setting – usually over a meal – I like to go over a few principles with students.

One of the best experiences I've ever had with this was with a young friend of mine, Ameenah, who recently graduated high school. Her academic performance was excellent. She graduated salutatorian (the second ranked student in her class of 400) and was well-liked by her classmates.

No problems there.

But I found Ameenah to lack a bit of personal confidence and I wanted to just reinforce that a bit before she headed off to school on scholarship.

After giving her a graduation present and engaging in a little bit of girl talk, I told my brilliant young mentee that there was something I wanted to give her even more valuable than the beauty salon gift certificate, magazine subscriptions, and eBook reader I had earlier placed in her hands.

"Let me show you something," I said.

Taking an unused napkin off of our table, I began to draw what looks like to many of my friends what is called the 'key' in basketball – the part in between the three point line and the basket, wherein free throws are attempted and where all dunks take place.

Since Ameenah played small forward on her high school basketball team, I made the comparison as I drew.

I had her full attention.

"I want to show you something that is important for you to understand as you go into business for yourself," I stated firmly.

In the semicircle area, I wrote the word "support base", and then divided the rectangular part underneath the semicircle into what now looked like bars. In each bar I wrote a different word: 'Turf'; 'Authority'; 'Expertise'; 'Charisma'; 'Subordinates'.

"Ameenah, all of those people who will help you, say good things about you, promote you, provide you information, and introduce you to people, are your support base. They may be family members, classmates, friends, co-workers and people you know in the neighborhood. We *never know all of the people in our support base.* But you want everybody in your personal network to be in it. You grow your network of supporters through the five elements of your power base.

"Your Turf represents the limits and boundaries, even, of what you aspire and dream about accomplishing. Ameenah, although people will tell you this to cheer you up and encourage you, there is no such thing as 'the sky is the limit.' Everyone has limitations on their power and influence and what they can accomplish. So you must know what they are. So, when you set goals, be clear on their boundaries and where success and failure lie. Do you want to be the most powerful person in the world, or just in your profession, school, community, or the neighborhood? Be clear on that.

"Your Authority simply refers to the rights and privileges you have, usually as a result of the position and roles you occupy in life. You have them as a person, business owner, citizen, employee, and family member. But they mainly refer to your formal roles in life.

"Your Expertise is all of the knowledge and insight you have. But not only that, but also *the reputation you have for being knowledgeable and for having insight that is relevant and useful.* It is not just what you actually know that gives you expertise. It is also what people *think* you know and how they react to you because of that perception and reputation.

"Your Charisma is your spirit, aura, personality; your level of attraction or magnetism. It is not only the sum of your personality-oriented powers and qualities of attraction and influence, but also your skill in knowing *when* to use or show those powers and qualities. It is knowing when to be sensitive and when to be tough; when to speak softly and when to speak more vocally; when to wear what, and how to 'speak the language' of different types of people.

"Your Subordinates are those people who will one day report to you, Ameenah, obey you, or are under your direct authority. These people get their own category because they are so important. The people who work for you, report to you, and are under your direct authority *reflect who you are*. In one way or another they represent and reveal the impact of how you use your power, for good or bad, when you are the one most in control of the relationship. And they appear in every area of your life - at work and home.

"Now in each of these five areas, which make up your Power Base, you have the ability to increase your personal power.

"By winning friends, doing good works, and influencing others positively you expand your Support Base. By studying yourself and others and being specific and clear on exactly what you do, you not only know every square inch of your Turf, but you know what parts of your Turf should concern you the most. Your Turf has a best part, a poor part and a worst part. By understanding the levels of Authority you possess, you can determine how to leverage the rights, privileges and prerogatives you are entitled to and presently enjoy. By learning – observing, reading, reasoning and experiencing – you increase your level of knowledge, wisdom, and understanding. And by understanding how and where others believe you are knowledgeable and ensuring that what you know is relevant and useful, you can increase your reputation for Expertise. By realizing what aspects of your personality and character make you attractive and influential in different scenarios, you can raise your level of Charisma. And finally, any time a person is under your care or authority you are in a relationship with a Subordinate that may become public. The proper handling and relating to those over whom you have power – those that look up to you, and who obey you, may be the ultimate measure of who you really are in life, and in the eyes of others. And remember, it is *who you are when no one is looking* that can matter the most."

I looked at Ameenah to see how she was taking it. She was in rapt attention, thinking and reflecting, but silent.

"Would you like to continue and learn more?" I asked, a bit curious about her silence.

"Yeah!" she replied, with energy in her voice, yet leaning back.

We ordered desert and then I went further.

"Now, once you have the five aspects of your Power Base down, you have to begin to understand the five Power Types and Sources," I resumed, with confidence and enthusiasm.

"There are five Power Sources and Types: 'Coercive'; 'Reward'; 'Legitimate'; 'Expert'; and finally, 'Associative/Referent'.

"Coercive Power is the ability that one has to punish or frustrate some need of another, to compel someone to do something. For example, I may have food while you are with me and you are hungry, practically starving. Then I choose to deny you that unless you do something on my behalf. Police and the governments have this form of power. They can make or compel you to do things by force. It is also sometimes called punitive power. The best example of all, though, is that of parents. They have coercive power over their children. They can apply force to direct the will of their babies and young children." I said.

Laughing with understanding, Ameenah blurted out, "Tell me about it!"

I smiled, totally re-connecting to what it feels like to be a teenager.

"Reward Power is driven a lot by incentives," I continued.

"You can also see this with parents in their relationship with a young child. Instead of using physical force they may say, 'If you go to bed now, I will read you a bedtime story.' If you work for someone you also can see Reward Power. In exchange for work, your company pays you a salary. They may also have a bonus available in order to give you an incentive to reach a certain level of performance.

"Legitimate Power is the power that one has as a result of their authority by title or position. They might be a department chair at a University. A supervisor at work. A teacher in a classroom. Or a military officer in uniform in a community under martial law. In some cultures people receive power based upon a title or class structure. In some cultures and organizations there are strict levels or hierarchies where positions are not challenged - power runs up a chain of command, but not down. Interestingly, among those who have been historically oppressed and discriminated against, this is the form of power sought after the most.

"Expert Power is that which comes with having special knowledge or expertise. Some experts have the attitude of, 'I know how to do this so you must depend upon me.' Sometimes this is true, but that depends upon the other person. Remember what I said earlier about expertise. For it to be a real form of power another person has to accept it and *see you* as knowledgeable and worthy of advising others. But you have to have that *reputation*. Because experts are really advisers they depend upon others to have a need for what they know. Very powerful people know how to utilize and manage experts.

"Associative/Referent Power is the power that derives from an association. This power can exist when one has access or a relationship to a powerful person. The very best example I could give you is that of the Reverend in the Christian tradition (or an Imam in Islam or a Rabbi in Judaism) who claims to know or represent God. But we all have this power based upon our relationships and access to others who are perceived as powerful or having that which others need or want. By associating ourselves with other powerful people we can gain influence. Another good example would be the many companies that sell products by using celebrities in television commercials. The endorsement of the celebrity can give credibility to the product or make it attractive.

"Can you see the big picture of Power now, Ameenah?" I inquired.

"Yeah, but I never saw it this clearly before, you know what I mean?" was her reply.

"I understand. It really is a wonderful way of thinking and looking at yourself and the world," I stated.

"How did you come up with all of this?" she asked.

I looked her directly in the eyes and said, "Through all of my travels in life – I have been sensitive to these relationships. I see them at work in business, in social settings – even in this restaurant we are in, and I can reflect over moments filled with these dynamics in childhood. It is always present in the relationships we have, for better or worse, each day. All that I have done in this particular area, that you haven't yet, and which almost no one does, because we aren't taught to, is *organize the knowledge I have gained from just living and learning.* If you are able to do this and apply it to everyday realities, and recognize the power that you do and don't have, and how to get it, you will be successful in life, my friend.

"And much of this of course is based upon my professional training. What I have studied about power is documented and publicly available but *I* brought something to what I studied – my own experience, values, and perspective. So while I have organized it maybe in a unique way, I want to make clear to you that I learned much of this from others. It comes a lot from my professional career and personal development - stuff I have read; conferences I've attended, and people I've met in different settings and the interpretations on life and circumstances they've shared with me."

"Can I keep that?" she asked so innocently, as if she were a little girl, half her age.

"Of course!" I replied, folding it up neatly, then placing it in her gift bag.

I tended to my desert and took care of the check, giving her some time to let it all sink in.

And then, after laying down a tip, my 18-year old high school graduate shocked me with this statement, expressed more clearly than anything I had stated over the last 2 hours, "It seems like people underestimate their own power, while overestimating the power of others. But no matter how much we understand it, we all have it and want more of it, in some way. I don't think that's bad or good, I just think it's *real*."

I had accomplished my mission. Whether Ameenah ever used that napkin again, she got the bottom line.

"Come on girl, let's go shopping!" I announced.

I was not done sharing.

And judging by how quickly she got up out of her chair and put her coat on, Ameenah was ready to receive.

# Chapter 5: Etiquette: Manners and Networking Do Matter

"Good manners are made up of petty sacrifices."

**- Ralph Waldo Emerson**

"Manners are a sensitive awareness of the feelings of others. If you have that awareness, you have good manners, no matter which fork you use."

**- Emily Post**

"I've never been here before," Ameenah told me as we pulled into the parking lot of a plaza full of boutique stores in another part of town.

"That's what I figured, but don't worry, you will be coming back here over and over again, I'm pretty sure. Now tell me, what is it you think you are going to major in?" I asked.

"Well, they don't let you pick until you enter the School of Business in your 3rd year of college. But I want to be an accountant right now." She stated, making it clear no final decision had been made.

"Well, you have time to figure that out. But what we won't wait any longer for is your learning a few basics in what is called professional dress and business etiquette," I told her.

"What's that?" she asked, realizing this shopping trip may not be as fun as she may have first thought.

"It's just big words that mean knowing what to wear, what to say, and what to do when you are trying to get things done in whatever field you decide to work in. The first thing I want to show you is over here," I said as I pointed to a section of the store we had walked into, where business card holders were showcased.

"It may be a bit too early for you to use this on a regular basis, but one day you'll be pulling out your business card as much as you pulled out your school I.D. this year. So I want you to get comfortable with that and the first step is buying the right kind of card holder. Like this one, here," I said while grabbing a nicely stitched leather business card holder.

Placing the card holder in her hand as I walked toward another section of the store, I added, "Hold on to it. I'll explain more about how important it is."

"What are you doing?" she asked, as we stopped at a counter and a store clerk handed me a garment bag full of clothes.

"Oh nothing, just picking up a week's worth of clothes for you to try on for when you have to attend events and meetings, or even go to work, in what is called a 'business casual' environment," as I began to lay out skirts, slacks, pant suits, and blouses.

"Try these on over here," were my last words before opening a dressing room door for her.

"I'm buying you clothes in a 'business casual' style, because I know you have nothing like them in your wardrobe. It is one of the subtle things you have to learn about the world of business. Little things can mean so much, you know. Here, read this before you try all of this stuff on," I said as I slipped a piece of paper – an article - under her door.

What I gave her would make clear what I meant by 'little things':

**Dress for Work Success: A Business Casual Dress Code**
**By Susan M. Heathfield, About.com Guide**

Your Company's objective in establishing a business casual dress code, is to allow our employees to work comfortably in the workplace. Yet, we still need our employees to project a professional image for our customers, potential employees, and community visitors. Business casual dress is the standard for this dress code.

Because all casual clothing is not suitable for the office, these guidelines will help you determine what is appropriate to wear to work. Clothing that works well for the beach, yard work, dance clubs, exercise sessions, and sports contests may not be appropriate for a professional appearance at work.

Clothing that reveals too much cleavage, your back, your chest, your feet, your stomach or your underwear is not appropriate for a place of business, even in a business casual setting.

Even in a business casual work environment, clothing should be pressed and never wrinkled. Torn, dirty, or frayed clothing is unacceptable. All seams must be finished. Any clothing that has words, terms, or pictures that may be offensive to other employees is unacceptable. Clothing that has the company logo is encouraged. Sports team, university, and fashion brand names on clothing are generally acceptable.

Certain days can be declared dress down days, generally Fridays. On these days, jeans and other more casual clothing, although never clothing potentially offensive to others, are allowed.

The article then went on to detail suggestions on business casual dressing for work – covering everything from slacks, pants, pant skirts, dresses, skirted suits, shirts, tops, blouses, jackets, shoes, jewelry, makeup, perfume, cologne, hats and head covering.  It ended with this stern conclusion, "If clothing fails to meet these standards, as determined by the employee's supervisor and Human Resources staff, the employee will be asked not to wear the inappropriate item to work again. If the problem persists, the employee may be sent home to change clothes and will receive a verbal warning for the first offense. All other policies about personal time use will apply. Progressive disciplinary action will be applied if dress code violations continue."

After 45-minutes of what felt like a fashion show, Ameenah and I left the store – placed the items that fit in the trunk, and then went to the nearby coffee shop, where I wanted to talk further with her.

We exchanged few words while walking and in line.

Once we had fresh beverages, I began, "I know you want to become an accountant but there is a whole culture to doing business that can sometimes matter as much or more than the balance sheets, business plans, audits, and how much money may be at stake in your regular work. The way you do business, what you wear, how you conduct yourself around others – and knowing what *not* to say or do at certain times can determine whether deals get done and ultimately whether you accomplish your objective. With our time together today I wanted to impress upon you the importance of these kinds of things.  I just used the basics like – a meal, a business card, and your attire to make a few points." I responded, striving for a calm sense of thoughtfulness I wanted her to feel.

"Would you mind sharing with me more of what you've learned in this area?" she responded so humbly.

Laughing I replied "Sure, I had some notes ready for you, hoping you'd be interested!"

"Remember," I started, "the big thing about etiquette and networking in business that I'm stressing is that *you* represent your plan, idea, product, or service.  Your appearance, conduct and conversation matter as much as the other obvious factors in business.

"Isn't it striking, Ameenah, that we can work hard to create a reputation, image, product or plan after hours, days and even years of hard work and striving, but the *presentation* of it is not of the same quality. It's like studying for a test for a month and then deciding to guess at the answers when you finally take it. We just don't tend to put as much energy, effort and attention to detail in the representation of ourselves, the agenda, and the business product and service, as we do other areas of the process.

"But look at how important this is. When you are presenting something you are introducing it, offering it, or bringing it into view, often for the first time. And that word 'time' is very important because in today's society we don't have much of it, especially when you are dealing with people who recognize that time is money or the opportunity to make money.

"That is why I took you to buy the business card holder. It is usually part of your first impression. You need to communicate unspoken things to people quickly, in order to save time. If you have met someone and have a great conversation about what you might be able to do for, and with them, and you have conveyed an image of professionalism and orderliness *and then* you reach into your pocket and pull out a stack of cards with a rubber band around it, with their edges bent, the presentation becomes less than representative of what you are trying to convey. Your representation is now disruptive.

"This distracts, interferes with and takes away from the transmission, clarity or quality of what we are trying to send or receive. Ameenah, it's a shame to have spent so much time working on something like a great idea, plan, or project, only to lose out on an opportunity, because, in the presentation stage, we didn't dot our I's and cross our T's so to speak.

"And most people don't realize that their presentation is both informal and formal. A multi-colored rhinestone business card case *may* convey something acceptable in the music, entertainment or fashion industries but what it conjures up in the mind of the average person who sees it – who doesn't operate in those worlds – can work against you. You may not realize it but yes, something as small as a business card holder may challenge a positive reputation that your hard work or an endorsement has created. Being sloppy is not in harmony with a reputation for neatness and orderliness.

*"Your presentation should be as impressive as the information you are conveying.* What usually prevents that from happening is awkwardness. Awkwardness is the state that is created from not knowing where you are, how things work, being late, and doing or saying something inappropriate. Not knowing what fork to use. Not being organized. All of this creates a sense of awkwardness which can distract from your presentation.

"The key to avoiding awkwardness is preparation. If you have a meeting at a restaurant, go ahead of time. If you can afford it give a tip to the maitre d' – the hostess, head waiter or person in charge. Ask him or her where to sit. Know the menu in advance. Finding out that your guest is allergic, a vegetarian, or on a diet, ahead of time, can avoid awkwardness during the business meal.

"Ameenah, I hope you noticed how the clerk behind the counter at the store we just left already knew me and gave me the clothes as I approached the counter. I arranged that through preparation for our meeting today.

"In a business setting, you don't want distractions, so make sure that your attire and presence are in order – your glasses are not crooked or smeared; there are no spots on your clothes; your hair is in place.

"You know my hair has to be right, Ami!" Ameenah joked, giving me a high five as she spoke.

"You know it," I said "Nails too," as we both laughed.

I paused and smiled at her, appreciating her sense of humor before beginning again.

"We also should be aware of what colors convey. There is an art and science to this. Wearing neutral colors like brown, green and gray is usually a good decision. Black is a formal color in business. When you are at a meal you will want to come off as casual and make people comfortable. The same is true for group presentations. Browns, greens and grays are more relaxing. Black is formal. Red and yellow steal power - they take attention away from others and what you are presenting. Any 'loud' color steals power. Be careful with blues. Navy blues are like black, but off-blues are closer to gray. What determines whether something is considered too bold, relaxed, or formal are style and categories of colors. A person in business should learn what the scale is – from what is usually considered extremely bold like bright colors, seductive cuts, and high fashion on one end, to what is most commonly considered to be ultra formal, like wearing a black tie, on the other end.

"You always want to stay on top of what is considered proper etiquette and networking behavior by being observant, speaking to more experienced people, and by reading books, which are widely available, and articles on the subject. But all of that takes place inside of the larger picture that you are doing business and want to accomplish an objective. Two barriers: 1) ignorance and 2) an attitude of stubbornness, are people's worst enemies in this regard. Etiquette and networking customs and traditions are not about what you like, they are about what is considered the right thing to wear, say or do, and what the most likely interpretation will be to how you appear, and what you say or do.

"This does not mean that you can't personalize and add style, but you have to be honest about whether you are doing this for yourself alone or for the person you are seeking to convey something to, on behalf of your business objective.

"Fashion is about personality, awareness, identity and branding.

"Look at Presidents, there is not much deviation in their standard way of dressing. All Presidents seem to wear basically the same five ties, never too bold or outrageous. Why? Presidents want to convey something. They want to appear steady, confident, reassuring, and powerful.

"Regardless to what your profession, or the industry your business is in, there is an easy way to remember what matters in terms of appearance. Keep this rule in mind: *your appearance is part of your presentation and needs to be planned, contrived, consistent, and comfortable.*

"Let me say something about each, OK? But your coffee is getting cold – let me get you a refill." I said, wanting to give Ameenah a small break.

"Thanks…this is so much, can I take notes?" she asked politely.

"Here," I said, after reaching into my purse for my notepad and pen.

"Fresh brew or a latte this time?' I inquired.

"Vanilla latte, please Ami, thanks" she said, so deep in thought I at first thought she hadn't heard me.

While in line I thought about stopping altogether but I just could not take the risk of assuming I would have her attention like this again.

Sadly, I realized going over the ins and outs of networking and etiquette with a teenager may be a once-in-a-lifetime opportunity.

<<<<>>>>

Dragging out the fixing of my own cup of coffee a bit longer than normal, I returned with Ameenah's hot latte.

"Ok, now you have to keep sipping while I talk this time, sorry for talking so much." I offered.

She smiled and then said, "No, I'm ready for more. I can drink and write."

"Alright, here we go, let's get into the key to knowing how to present yourself in different settings, and creating an image, reputation and personal brand that are in harmony," I remarked, pulling out of a notebook some prepared notes as if making a speech.

"*Planned:* Do your homework about what is appropriate and what is not. A cookout demands something a black tie affair does not. Colors and style should be planned.

"*Contrived:* You should be rehearsing what you wear and experiencing how it feels and looks on you, and how you move in it. Try the garment on ahead of time. Don't wait until the morning of to learn the outfit is too tight, not complimentary to your build, or showing too much body form or cleavage.

"*Consistent:* Maintain your image. Realize your past appearances are creating an image. Be consistent because everything you do reinforces or detracts from that. Being inconsistent can therefore become your consistent image. Do you want that? The level of comfort of the people you are attempting to do business with is the target you are trying to hit and remember no style *is* a style. Think of Russell Simmons. He has been known for years for wearing a baseball cap and suit with no tie to all kinds of occasions. Fine. But when he takes the baseball cap off it causes confusion. Some will like it and some will dislike it. It's noticed and perhaps that is what he wants. You've got to be aware of that reaction in making your decision and accept there will be disapproval and fallout. There is going to be that push back and negativity and discomfort coming from and experienced by others when someone becomes inconsistent in appearance, contrary to an established image that they have created. But to what degree that resistance is properly managed is the key. When the change in appearance is instant, or too fast, the consequences can be dramatic. The statement *you* are trying to make or whatever *you* may think of yourself, does not change the reality that your appearance is going to constantly be evaluated in terms of the existing standards of what is considered appropriate and suitable to the circumstance. And if you are willing to go against those standards and customs you must be willing to accept it. For a long time, casualness went with creativity, and the more casual artists appeared, the more creative they were considered to be in some circles. But some artists have broken that mold and started wearing suits.

"In hip-hop this happened over the years with Jay-Z. He now has achieved a very respected business image through his change in wardrobe and subtle things he does through fashion. He has very successfully established an image, brand, and reputation that is in harmony with his personality and business objectives. Russell Simmons felt his appearance made his audience more comfortable and helped them perceive him as younger than he really was. But some people said he was trying *too hard* to be young or hip. It was a negative, perhaps, but not too much of a negative, because of how he managed the reaction – with spoken and unspoken things. And he was also sending a message to another audience – his core group of supporters who may have respected his defiance - by *not wearing* what he was supposed to. That may have been good for business in terms of the sale of his products and services. It strengthened his brand, perhaps. But again, especially when you are not established yet, simply looking good and feeling correct is not the issue – but being *appropriate* is. The dullest looking thing to you may be the most appropriate to 'them'. I know someone who refused to wear company blazers because they felt they were corny, but from a corporate culture standpoint his *not* wearing the company's blazer was *inappropriate*. He dressed for himself but not in the best interests of his professional and business objectives.

"*Comfortable:* If your own discomfort with what you must wear in order to be appropriate gets to the level of awkwardness, then you may need to practice and rehearse wearing that attire. Look at female entertainers who wear stilettos and dance and move around. They got that way because they rehearsed and practiced so that they would be comfortable and appropriate. Look at models. They have to practice a way to walk until it becomes comfortable. A person who has to wear shirts and ties and doesn't like to needs to learn to hate it less. It takes practice to feel less awkward. It is easy to be in your own comfort zone and harder to get into another person's, but if you want something from them, you better do what you need to in order to *get* into their comfort zone. It's about selling. The best way to sell is to make other people comfortable. And you can learn to become less uncomfortable by practicing, rehearsing, and acting. Practice, drill, rehearse, act, and look in the mirror and ask others how you look. That's how you gain comfort - through practice.

"So remember Ameenah: it's all about having it <u>planned</u>, <u>contrived</u>, <u>practiced</u>, <u>consistent</u> and <u>comfortable</u>," I concluded.

"Now that we've dealt a bit with appearance, I want to share my thoughts about business meals with you." I said gently.

"OK, this is very important I already know, and my parents are always getting on my brother and I about our table manners," she eagerly replied.

<<<<>>>>

"Many, many business decisions are made over meals. In business settings these are power breakfasts, power lunches, banquets, receptions, brunches, and coffees. The reason is that food makes people more relaxed and comfortable. It evens out the bar for people to communicate. A CEO eats a hot dog the same way as a clerk. Meals are a great equalizer – we are all people and generally eat the same way. Throughout just about any culture you could imagine, food is comforting and affects our mood and emotional state. The same is true for beverages like water, tea, coffee and alcohol. A whole culture and a large body of customs and traditions have developed around food and beverages," I started our new topic.

"Therefore, the location of a business meeting is important, whether a hotel banquet room, restaurant, lounge, coffee shop, bar, or club. In meeting at these places have a plan and be clear on your objectives. If I want to talk to you about a project and have to get you away from your office and other people by inviting you out for coffee, I should first find out that you actually do like coffee. And if I learn that you don't, there should be other beverages available that you do enjoy. I should also make sure the available beverages are appropriate for drinking during business hours on a work day – and usually alcohol is not. Keep in mind that the setting must be appropriate and conducive. You don't want to go to a noisy or crowded place. The food and beverage should not be a distraction. It should be supportive and positively impressive.

"I must also plan what I am going to say to you and *when*, because we are not going somewhere to get together just for coffee, or talk about the weather, or critique the restaurant. There is something that I, you, or we, need to ask one another or get clarification on, arriving at an understanding together through conversation.

"But it's important not to rush things. Don't start the meal with the business at hand. Just work into that. Talk about the food and enjoy the environment. Don't pull out the papers or proposal right away. The conversation should lead to what the objective is. If I want to tell you about a business plan, I normally wouldn't present it during the meal unless it is at the end. But try to not create an awkward moment by changing the mood and cluttering the environment. If you are skillful in operating a mobile phone that has the right features, perhaps there is something you can show a person that is large enough for them to see and easy enough for them to understand. The beauty of handheld devices is that you don't need to carry around a whole lot of stuff in a briefcase or binder anymore. Technology may allow you to show something on a phone or electronically, but you must be careful. The goal is to not distract and to not be awkward.

"Use the meal as an opportunity, perhaps, to arrange a more formal meeting later. This is if you are trying to get your foot in the door and get an audience. This might be considered a pre-presentation meal, or informal coffee talk.

"But a presentation may be expected as the purpose of the meeting. Sometimes the other party may want you to bring a plan and the meal is just an opportunity for them to get away to look it over. Just be clear about the expectations in advance. You have to know the difference between a pre-presentation meal and one where more detailed discussion about an opportunity and even the closing of a deal is the expectation or objective. Lay the groundwork for the right meal, if you are the one arranging it. Remember what I said earlier about doing some advance work ("The key to avoiding awkwardness is preparation. If you have a meeting at a restaurant, go ahead of time. Give a tip to the maitre d' – the hostess, head waiter or person in charge. Ask him or her where to sit. Know the menu in advance. Finding out that your guest is allergic, a vegetarian, or on a diet can create awkwardness"). To have the kind of meeting you want, you will have to take the initiative and lay the groundwork for it.

"And of course you have to be mindful of the time. A breakfast meeting probably means you know the person has to get somewhere else after they meet with you. Lunchtime is always limited and meals during the evening face the reality that people want to get home at a reasonable hour. So, you may only have only an hour or 90 minutes, max.

"Now at a more formal meal – a group meal with others - the goal is making a first, lasting, memorable, distinct and differentiating impression. This is where branding comes in. Make sure your appearance represents you and not an inappropriate image – tie not shuffled, blouse too low, or suit not pressed.

"When at group tables, proper etiquette is important. There are basic rules to follow - know the table settings and manners, and no talking while the keynote speaker is making remarks.

"What you were taught about table manners at home, if at all, will help at formal group meals, but it won't be enough. You need to practice and do research on formal dinner settings and proper table manners. Get a book on etiquette or read one at a public library. Ask others with more experience than you, too. The goal is always to be prepared to avoid awkward or distracting moments.

"You may be surprised how detailed a formal dinner can be. Some etiquette classes I have attended show as many as 28 pieces on the table. But there are some basic things to remember:

- Your drinking glasses are always on the right

- Your bread plate or saucer is always on the left and is where 'everything' goes – chewing gum, butter, paper, wrappings, seeds

- Many table setting plates are for decoration only and are not to be eaten on or used during the meal

- Eat using utensils positioned from the outside in. With each course – appetizer, soup, salad, main course, desert – you work your way in, starting from the outer utensil

- When you pass food around it is always to your left

"In some cultures like European, etiquette is actually publicly taught. Caribbean and African based cultures teach this at home. In America, etiquette is frequently an afterthought.

"And there are appropriate ways to stand out. An impressive move is to stand up and introduce yourself individually to each person at your table. This will show confidence and will make you memorable. It also avoids awkward and distracting moments like when you have to speak loudly, lean, or reach across people to make introductions or shake hands.

"And for males, when a woman approaches the table, they should stand up and pull her chair out for her. Allow her to signal whether it is necessary or not – but the key is that they will be acknowledged by her. Keep this in mind as a young lady, yourself.

"Something that I have seen lately that is a definite no-no at a formal meal is utilizing a mobile phone at the table. Don't text at the table. The same applies to taking a call. Put your phone on vibrate. As a general rule, if you have to look at something, read or write, just step away. There is nothing inappropriate about excusing yourself. Inappropriateness comes when you do not excuse yourself. It borders on rude. Pay attention to the current situation. If I am having dinner with you, that is all I should be doing. But if your focus is somewhere else, you are signaling that what you are doing with me is not that important to you. Show the person that you want to be there by being attentive.

"Think of how you feel when you come to somebody's office and they say – in front of you – to their secretary or executive assistant, 'Please take all of my calls. I don't want to be interrupted.' That is impressive and shows that you are really wanted there.

"When I have meetings and the phone rings, I don't even look at it. One thing at a time is my goal. I know how it makes a person feel to have somebody's full attention.

"I know that our common excuse is that we are 'multi-tasking', but people know that when you are doing something else in front of them you are not giving your full attention to them or their interests. You are disrespecting the meeting. If you are expecting an important call, set it up ahead of time by letting the person you are meeting with know about it in advance. It shows consideration.

"This is one of the challenges of new technology. There are more opportunities for us to be interrupted. We get so much information coming in to us that it is hard to concentrate on a single thing or person without a deliberate effort. But we have to balance the benefits of technology and its ability to keep us connected to information and our personal and professional network, with courtesy and respect for others.

"To keep a good frame of mind in this area, I think the question to ask would be: *how does it make you feel when someone does that to you*? With that perspective, you probably won't unnecessarily offend or slight someone else at a business engagement," I concluded my points.

"I bet you feel like you are in class don't you?" I asked, knowing she would nod as she did.

"I'm so sorry Ameenah, but I'm sharing this stuff with you this way because you, unfortunately, never had this in class. And neither did I when I was your age." I apologized, not only for myself, but it felt like also for an entire country.

<<<<>>>>

Surprised a bit at how much she had been paying attention to detail, Ameenah ended any fears I had about her being disinterested when she asked, "Ok, we've touched on appearance, business meals and formal dinners but what about conduct at conferences and conventions? I just attended a summer youth leadership conference where they dealt with some of it but they told us as we got older we would learn more about it. What are some things to keep in mind?" I asked.

I immediately responded, "Conventions and conferences, where people are more relaxed or open, are great opportunities to gather information and arrange future meetings. But that won't happen unless you follow through and follow up with the people you meet or make contact with at these events. As a general rule, take no more than two days to reach back out to whomever you may have met and remind them of the meeting, even informing them of what you have decided to do regarding what was previously discussed.

"A good thing to always remember to do is to write important details on the back of a person's business card. Write the event, the discussion, what was discussed, and who introduced you. And prior to any conference or convention get a business notepad, leather bound. They are good for these kinds of reminders for follow-through, especially since some people have business cards that are too narrow to write on. These slick and sleek cards are impressive but are really for appearance only and can't hold a lot of other information you may want to add to the card, so be prepared and get a business notepad.

"And here is where the kind of pen you use can matter in supporting the reputation, brand, or image you have established, or are seeking to establish. I believe that the only name that should be on the pen you use for a business purpose is your own name, or that of your company. No other name should be on a pen you use – not the hotel, or bank where you picked up the pen for free, and not another organization.

"And make sure the pen writes too. I've seen people with beautiful pens that don't write. They just look good!

"So our conversation goes back to me buying you your first business card holder today, because your pen and your business card holder are part of your presentation, especially at a conference and convention where you are meeting people for the first time. Investing in quality that you can afford will only impress. It will never detract from you.

"Leather is the most appealing texture for your business card holder. Never use metallic or plastic, or your wallet. Imagine someone struggling to pull a business card out of a wallet and they end up dropping other business cards, credit cards, receipts, and money in the process. Just think about the impression that might make on you. Is this the kind of message we are trying to send about our brand or image? Would that be consistent with everything else you were saying or doing in representing a great idea, quality product or professional ability?

"And give some thought to your business card, but not too much. What I mean is sometimes less is more. You don't need something extravagant, just something useful and appropriate. My favorite business card of all time was a mouse-trap that I received from an exterminator. It was memorable but not useful or appropriate. Other cards I remember, for all the wrong reasons, are the glossy colorful ones of an odd size. I can't write on them and they don't fit neatly into anything.

"The finish of your business card should allow someone to write on the back of it easily, and the dimensions should allow it to fit easily into a business card holder or compartment for business cards in a planner or business briefcase or professional bag.

"All people want in a business card is to know who you are, how to contact you, and what you do. If you do have a logo, great – stick it on the card and give people some space to write some details about your company, idea or a point or two made during conversation.

"If you are selling a personal service, a picture is appropriate on your business card but be careful of the message it sends. It is appropriate, if you want to be memorable in the right way. Remembering people you meet and being remembered is important in business. I have a friend and he is really clever. He takes a photo of people when he meets them and does it in a non-intrusive way. He attaches that photo to their name in his electronic phonebook so when they call him, their picture will come up and he will remember them. His goal is to remember people.

"But it is important to know who you are doing business with and how they may perceive (or misperceive the purpose of) a picture. If you have a picture on your card, inform the person that the purpose of it is so they will remember you. Explain it just in case the person doesn't understand why you have this on there. In some cultures it is inappropriate to put your picture on a business card. It seems egotistical. And definitely don't put other people's pictures on a card or on your professional profile page on a social media site.

"And this brings me to another point. In this era of 'new' media many of the rules of business etiquette still apply but others are being forgotten or re-written. There are things on community pages that we should be careful of and must think through. People can learn a lot about you on profile pages. Some of us, if we could start over again would tailor our profile pages to be less like our personal journal or diary, and more like our professional resumes.

"People should do their homework on those forums. Remember these are forums that anybody and everybody has access to: profile pages, blogs and search engines. They are valuable tools but if mismanaged, they can haunt you, and hurt you in business.

"My rule on popular community sites like Facebook is that *I'm responsible* for what is on my page. What I present and allow others in my network to comment on or add, is a reflection of me. But even then I can't be surprised, and shouldn't be surprised, if people whom I want to do business with form opinions of me, right or wrong, or for better or worse, through an impression of my social media pages. Everything up there is for public consumption and personal interpretation. So, you may be wondering, would it be wise to just stay off of these kinds of websites and away from popular online forums and places where my opinions and image may be publicly accessible? Not necessarily. Because remember, no communication *is* communication. If you are not on these sites or in these forums it might suggest:

- You may be hiding something

- You are not up on technology

- You don't make time for something that might be able to help you professionally"

"You could actually hurt yourself by not having a presence in places like these, especially if you are in a technology related field where there is an expectation for you to be on the cutting edge and engaged or aware of trends. You don't want it to seem that you are not relevant or in tune." I said, in refining points made earlier.

<<<<>>>>

Feeling that we were where we needed to be, I decided to summarize some etiquette and networking steps and the process of succeeding in business or professionally when interacting within a different culture. I knew Ameenah could relate to this with both of us being raised in America but born to parents who were not.

"We have to learn to recognize, respect, understand and navigate our cultural differences. But there are more cultures than we usually recognize at first thought. There are organizational, ethnic, gender, geographic, religious, and generational cultures, just to name a few. And of course you have tribal and ethnic cultures around the world. But it should be noted that wherever you have a group of people in close proximity to one another you have a culture. You have individual and collective value systems, interests, and objectives around which people organize themselves and compete.

"But the good news is that there are always three steps in a process of engaging and succeeding within a culture and in successfully navigating cultural differences.

"The steps are imitating, assimilating, and innovating/originating. I'll go through each.

Imitating is the period of awareness and learning, in which you are increasing your knowledge and understanding of a culture.

Assimilating is the stage when you are adopting the culture as your own and when you are being absorbed and accepted into that broader cultural system.

Innovating/Originating is the period of time when, after imitation and assimilation, you begin to create your own culture or add style inside of an existing culture.

"For example, within a work organization, you have to know the culture, its values, and what is or is not acceptable. What are the norms? Do you call people by first names? Is the dress business attire? Do people take long, short or no lunches? To what degree do they socialize outside of work?

"And when socializing, we always have to be careful of what the cultural and individual norms for fun are. Getting drunk may be fun for some but not others.

"Study and research the culture, and talk to and observe the people.

"Cultures are complex and they intermingle. And people who are leaders within them have different perceptions and expectations, even stereotypes, working for or against them. Some of these perceptions, expectations and stereotypes are due to race or religion, and many are gender-based. An organization headed by a woman will usually operate differently than one led by a man. Women tend to follow the three steps with different style and at a different pace. When a woman takes over an organization she imitates the pre-existing culture and gets it all down, then she assimilates so it becomes natural and comfortable. And once that is established then she does it her way. Women are more careful and deliberate about it, I find, because they often operate under greater scrutiny and stereotypes.

"The most impressive leaders are those who respect the three-step process of navigating cultural differences and are able to guide an organization properly through its evolution, and the impact of external forces. These leaders have a feel of how to pace themselves and the organization, and know where they and others are at in the process of imitation, assimilation, and origination.

"Look at President Obama, Ameenah. He's a quick learner but he does not have disregard for the existing culture. He naturally originates or creates his own style, but only after he first imitates and assimilates.

"In order to be successful operating within or during a short- or long-term engagement of any organization, we have to be able to navigate this.

"Once we identify what the cultural differences are in the organization, then we have to put that alongside of our own personal value system. What can we accept about what this culture demands or expects of those within it or who have entered into it in order to obtain some benefit for themselves? And this can be a challenge because some of us aren't willing to change.

"So many of us have irreconcilable conflicts between our current value system and the culture within which we must work professionally and in business. This makes it impossible for us to succeed.

"For instance, how can you run a business – an organization where profits and revenue generation determine success and survival and where people expect to be compensated – if you believe money is the root of all evil?

"How can you aspire to become a great entrepreneur if deep down you believe that any sign of accomplishment or success is evil, greedy, or bad? Why would you pursue something that is bad? If you think rich people are evil, then how are you going to become rich? You would not want to be rich.

"Etiquette and effective networking is a challenge for some, because how far can a person go in an organization or in promoting themselves if their value system won't allow them to get out of their comfort zone and socialize? Or what about those people who aren't willing to even follow recognized table manners because their value system so strongly prioritizes individuality and standing out or 'not being told what to do'?

"The entrepreneurs and professionals who are going to survive the current economic crisis that is requiring us to change organizations and suddenly interact with different cultures, are those who can imitate, assimilate, and originate because their value systems are not contradictory or in conflict with their identity and what they want to achieve in life.

"These kinds of persons will understand that politics are part of any and every organization and that we are just more comfortable dealing with it in some places than in others.

"These kinds of persons will understand the difference between *demonstrating* loyalty and *being* personally loyal. They know that *demonstrating* loyalty is a business dynamic, not a spiritual requirement. It is the ability to demonstrate attachment, support, and connection. Politicians can switch parties and still win elections. Coaches can leave football, soccer, hockey, basketball and baseball teams and win championships with different teams. CEOs can leave to go to new companies in a very short period of time and lead organizations full of people they have never worked with before, and in fact, have competed intensely against only days, weeks and months before. Entrepreneurs can set up businesses in different countries selling products to consumers because they know how to *demonstrate* loyalty, even if they have more personal loyalty to a particular political party, company, or country.

"This is because these persons are able to demonstrate to others what they may not feel exclusively or deeply within their hearts. These people know how to imitate, assimilate and originate and produce a consistent and reliable quality result regardless of time, place and circumstance.

"There is a difference between wearing a brand proudly and feeling proudly about a brand.

"I believe that at office parties, and drinks after work, you should be wearing the brand of the company you work for proudly, or demonstrating some form of loyalty to it. That is different than feeling proud about it. If you work for Nike, then many things in your wardrobe should have its symbol on it. But some people will say 'I'm not working for the company on off hours.' But they are confused. No one is asking them to feel something but rather only to *demonstrate* the feeling.

"This is a form of socialization – a business tactic that can be used in an environment different from the company workplace. Socialization is a way to break more effectively into a culture, gather information, or to get a point across. Galas, golf outings, elk clubs, spas, dance classes are more and more becoming socializing venues – places for networking and business meetings.

"If we are going to succeed in business we are going to more and more have to learn how to practice subordination and socialization.

"For example, if you go to a networking event and a Vice President of a company you really want to meet is present, but they are pre-occupied with five people around them, what can you do to get their attention and make an impression? A tactic you can use that is almost certain to work, if that Vice-President is drinking, is to identify the beverage they have, and go and get a new glass of it for them. Then, walk over to them and introduce yourself, while offering the refreshment.

"Subordination is a skill. But we call it brown-nosing, kissing up, or even something worse. Even if you take the stereotypes and negative values away from it, you can use humility and service as a powerful skill to get what you want. Subordination can be effective because it feels good to the receiver. If someone goes to get you a drink, find a seat for you, or take you away from a stressful situation, it makes you feel good.

"You can build so much cultural capital by doing this within an organization and it is a great way to stand out when networking, meeting the people who could be your next investor, business partner or employer.

"Another reason why socialization skills are important is because they may be your only opportunity to create a new image and brand for yourself, while working within an organization where a change in its hierarchy or structure is rare; when advancement from the bottom up is uncommon; and when you are interacting with people who may only see you in a certain way or who don't know you that well.

"It helps you to display what I call your 'invisible strengths' – those qualities that qualify you for greater responsibility, higher salary, or an investment. Many of us hold leadership positions outside of work: in our religious communities, sororities, fraternities, and even our families. Keep in mind people don't know this side of you until you share it or they observe it in action.

"So ask yourself if an employer, potential business partner or investor, or just anyone I want in my support base knew my invisible strengths, how would that impact the current image, reputation, and brand I have in their eyes?

"Sometimes those things that may be the least glamorous can qualify us for a responsibility far beyond what we hold now, and give people the confidence to entrust us with great authority and wealth. We often have hands-on experience that makes us valuable. This was one of President Obama's strengths in the 2008 campaign. He had hands-on experience as a community organizer. He'd been in the streets. He demonstrated that community and outreach skills can be transferable and valuable.

"I'll give you an example that applies specifically to entrepreneurs. Say you are planning to open up a supermarket in a poor community and you are trying to raise money for your venture. Having lived in that community or worshiped or visited relatives there frequently could be a plus in the eyes of an investor. They know you know the lay of the land, the language and style of the people, and the power centers in the neighborhood. Your invisible strengths and cultural capital would be an important consideration because it might positively impact the day-to-day operations and bottom line success in the business in that particular area.

"This has nothing to do with political ideology or whether he is a Republican or Democrat or neither. President Obama's cultural abilities are tremendous. Look at his background, travels, family members and ties and associations all over the world. He understands differences and how to navigate them. His socialization skills are perhaps better than anybody we have seen in his career path," I stressed the point.

"Well this is why I want you to appreciate all of these things and I spent so much time on them today, because it may be the last time I will be able to see you like this," I said, feeling a bit sad.

Knowing we had reached a great moment in our day, I officially concluded the business discussion.

"So enough of this before you make me cry," I said, joking a bit, as if Ameenah had *done something to me*. "Let's get you back home."

I felt good about what we had accomplished and although I knew she would not retain everything we discussed, I sincerely tried to make a lasting investment in someone's life – a person whom I cared about and whom I recognize faces greater opportunities and obstacles than I ever did.

*I know* I will see a return on that 'investment' one day. All I have to do is keep living and staying in touch with her, long enough to witness her exciting life path.

Not just me, but an entire world, would one day see her continued growth, I thought to myself – whether Ameenah ended up as an accountant or not.

Personal power, networking and etiquette skills can make *anyone* a success, and in any field.

# Chapter 6: Everyone Needs a Good Team

"Individual commitment to a group effort - that is what makes a team work, a company work, a society work, a civilization work."

**- Vince Lombardi**

"Never doubt that a small group of thoughtful, committed people can change the world. Indeed, it is the only thing that ever has."

**- Margaret Meade**

"Ms. Desai, I'm so sick of this! They're making me do all of the work on this, and it's not fair.  It's not right if I fail because of them."

This is what I was hearing from Michael – a student I've known for years who had come a long way – steadily improving in every area over the last two years.  Whether class participation, homework completion or test scores, his rate of progress in each area looked like a swift car on a steep ramp – headed upward fast, despite the pull of gravity.

He's a natural leader, with good manners, well-liked by classmates and easily one of the most popular students in all of school.

Yet, here he was, barging into my office in between class, without even giving me the slightest warning or greeting.

"Well, hello to you, too, Michael!" was my half-sarcastic response to the invasion of privacy and interruption.

"I'm sorry Ms. Desai, but I had to come see you before you left today, and in between 5$^{th}$ and 6$^{th}$ period is the only time I'm near your office.

But I gotta' talk to you about the business project we are working on because it's not going right with the partners when we are outside of school," He said, exasperated.

"What do you mean? I just sat in on the class the other day and you all said everything was going fine," I responded, bewildered.

'That's the problem. When we are in class, everything is fine. But when we agree to do things on our own no one comes through like they say. I'm tired of weeks of meeting at the coffee shop, my house, their house, over the computer and just talking…

"Ok, why are you smiling? I'm going to get an F and you are smiling. I'm not playing. I'm serious Ms. Desai."

I was not really smiling out of happiness or joy at what Michael was sincerely sharing.

It was just that he was so perfectly articulating a problem that millions of people experience in entrepreneurship – the lack of motivation and harmony among business partners.

"I'm not laughing at you Michael, I'm only smiling because I know exactly how you feel and because what you are going through *is* an important part of the project. It's a good thing!" I stated.

"What?!?" he said.

"Yeah, I'll explain it to you later, if you come by my office, after school. Don't worry about it. We'll talk," I said trying to intrigue as much as comfort.

"Alright," a skeptical but resigned Michael said heading – probably late – to his 6th period class.

<<<<>>>>

In some ways Michael had stumbled upon a dilemma and possible flaw in the course on entrepreneurship we had structured for the high school juniors and seniors. The objective of the 8 month program is for 11th grade students to partner with one another and formulate a business idea and then plan it successfully, with the help of mentors and experts that we bring in periodically to consult. The culmination of the project is the student groups' presentation of their ideas and plans for evaluation and possibly actual funding by a group of angel investors made up of representatives and members of the local chamber of commerce, venture capital and private equity firms and commercial banks.

The 11th graders are to design their businesses in a manner where they could actually open them during their 12th grade year, and are offered the option of seed capital or internships in a regional business related to the one they desired to start.

Michael, as an 11th grader, was now knee-deep, it sounded, wrestling with the sometimes unpleasant dynamic of interpersonal relationships that often sink businesses before or even soon after they have launched.

Those of us who planned the business and entrepreneurship course saw some of this coming but thought it would be better to develop *supplemental* materials to *guide teachers* in helping the students to deal with these issues.

We thought it may be a bit too much for the students to receive this material directly – fearing it would only aggravate the tension among them.

But now, Michael's reaction had me wondering – *were other students having this same problem but finding no place in the course where they'd have a chance to deal with it?*

Feeling a bit unsure, I went to visit one of the teachers instructing the course, Mrs. Jackson, and see if anything was up.

<<<<>>>>

"Hey Ami, how are you?" she said greeting me with her always beautiful smile, but clearly busy with a stack of papers on her desk. It looked like she was grading essays.

"Sorry to bother you, Tina, but I just got a frantic visit from Michael that prompted me to come ask you something," I gingerly raised the subject.

"Michael? What's wrong, is he OK?"

"Oh no, he's fine," I said. "I didn't mean to alarm you. He's just very upset over the lack of cooperation from his business partners in the project and it surprised me because by all appearances – just last week – everything looked fine," I revealed.

The look on Mrs. Jackson's face was a telling one; as if I now finally was 'in' on something.

"Ami, thanks for coming to me about this. I didn't know that about Michael, but there were a few incidents that I just became aware of with two of the groups. It seems that some heated arguments have been taking place about sharing the load equally and people feeling they deserve credit for certain ideas and progress and connections being made."

I immediately responded, "Right – he didn't go into that much detail because he was in between class but that's basically what Michael was alluding to. Now, I told him to come back and see me and I'm tempted to share with him some of the insights we had prepared for this. But the more I think about it, I wasn't so sure if that was the right thing to do away from your class activity and without involving you."

"No, it's OK with me Ami. You two have a good relationship and you can tell me how it goes. If he seems to grasp the concepts, I think maybe we should spend a few classes on the material we've been circulating among ourselves," Mrs. Jackson offered warmly.

"Thank you so much Tina, I'll let you know how it goes, tonight, if I can call you later."

"Sure, I cannot wait to hear from you on this one!" she said, expressing what both of us were sensing – Michael may be helping us make a decision we had not been able to arrive at on our own.

<<<<>>>>

A tired and pre-occupied Michael plopped down on the couch in my office, after school.

There was no need to ask first, I simply poured him a cup of ice cold water.

"Well, I'm glad you came to me earlier about the problem. You are bringing up an issue that we all are going to need to deal with – one way or another. I just want you to relax and tell me what's been going on," I said with as much reassurance as possible.

"Ms. Desai, they just don't have any idea about how to do this. They're lazy, unmotivated, slow and scared," Michael, told me in exasperation.

He then described, in detail, his efforts with four other classmates to get a music industry-related business off of the ground and ready for presentation to the angel group, and the challenges they faced – not only in researching and planning but in deciding who would do what and when. To his surprise and major disappointment, the most difficult aspects of what the team had embarked upon had little to do with what Michael initially thought would be roadblocks – figuring out the money, overcoming self doubt, and finding good information about how recording contracts are negotiated in the years since the Internet changed the way music was sold.

"This is *crazy*. *We* went over what everybody's role would be and even made clear how we were going to deal with the money when it came in. But even though we are supposed to be *equal* partners, I'm the one who has to stay on top of everybody, to make sure they do stuff. If I don't, nobody keeps their word or follows through."

I listened with sympathy, but could not help but smile and laugh to myself – these students were more than ready for a subject we adults had tried to 'shield' them from, or introduce gradually.

I could not make light of Michael's frustrations but I had to let him know, after he let off a bit more steam, that this was normal and would not come as a surprise again once he understood a few things about people.

"I mean, I thought we were partners, but these guys act as if *they are on a summer job*, waiting on somebody to give them orders. We all devoted time, energy and even a little bit of money to this project but our teamwork and effort is next to nothing!" Michael exclaimed.

Now was my chance.

I broke in before he could get rolling again.

"Relax, I know exactly how you feel. I went through this myself and I see it over and over again. Let me break a few things down for you," I interjected.

"If your vision is going to come true you are going to have to accept some realities about how people really are, from the inside out, not how they appear from the outside in. People will tell you *anything* when it comes to going into business for themselves. I mean, be honest, who really, nowadays wants to say *they don't* want the status and rewards that come from owning a business and building something from the ground up? It is something that we value nowadays, especially your generation, right?" I asked him.

"Yeah," he said with a sigh.

I continued, "But the reality is that not everybody's head and heart are in the place they need to be in order to do something for themselves. And not everyone has the same personality and temperament. So you can't go by what a person tells you, you have to go by their words, their actions, their mentality, personality, skills and talent. I don't like labeling or stereotyping people but I do believe that when it comes to entrepreneurship and business, people usually fall into a few categories. Want me to explain how it usually works?"

"Yes, Ms. Desai," Michael said almost sounding depressed. "Please explain this to me, because this isn't working out."

"Alright, give me a few minutes to go through this," I requested. "I think you will see your team in what I am about to lay out."

Now *I was the one* who needed some ice cold water as I reached into my mind, for memories, anecdotes and insights I gained from a variety of experiences and lessons I had learned, adapting the supplementary material to put it in a language Michael (and I now decided the entire class) would find easy to grasp and remember.

"Well, you have to know there are at least nine types of people that we are basically going to encounter when we find ourselves in business with partners. They all have their own strengths and weaknesses.

"They are 1) The Hustler 2) The Gangster..." at this point I was interrupted by laughter from Michael, which relieved me.

"I can't believe you – as a Headmaster of a school – are talking like this! But that's how us kids label people too," Michael explained, elated it seemed, that what looked like a lecture coming from me, might actually end up being be a good conversation.

"I'm glad, Michael, and that means that maybe you younger people have a lot to teach us older folks. But this isn't name-calling. These are just titles that will help you see qualities about people and how to tell the difference in business." I said, totally agreeing with him but trying to make sure he appreciated that there was a method to the terminology so that these labels would not be used as word-weapons by he or any of the other students.

"Ok, so next we have 3) The Entrepreneur 4) The Businessperson 5) The Professional 6) The Salesperson 7) The Ideologue 8) The Engineer and 9) The Coordinator. And all of them require a quick run-down. You will recognize some things when you hear me describe them. I promise, Michael.

"The Hustler is the person who can spot and perceive an opportunity to make money a mile away. Their mind is sharp and they tend to be good with numbers or weighing the risks and rewards or expenses and income in a situation. They are ambitious and confident but level-headed enough to turn down a situation that has money-making potential, but some red flags associated with it. Of all of the types of people out there, they are the most aggressive. They can literally sell anything. They have strong wills, and can persevere through all kinds of adversity in order to do business. They expect and anticipate difficulty and they embrace it – everyone needs some hustlers around them.

"But Hustlers have a few drawbacks. They tend to lose focus and concentration easily after they have completed a task and have what I call monetary attention deficit disorder (MADD). MADD is where you can't stop yourself from entertaining *any* opportunity to make money, even while you are already working on a project. Hustlers aren't sloppy but you might say they can be a bit greedy. They like to multi-task and because they can, they usually, sooner or later, get caught up in, well, a new hustle. Hustlers make money but they don't build businesses. They simply can't sit still long enough. And in their gut, they can't accept 'leaving money on the table'. If they think an opportunity is achievable, and there is enough reward for the risk, they won't be content with what they already have, they will seek more, and usually get it.

"The Gangster is a very important person to understand. They really have the entire package. They are professional, efficient, and patient in many respects. They know how to spot opportunities and they are exceptional at building an organization to pursue it. They understand power possibly better than any of the other eight types I am describing. The Gangster knows how to use charisma, expertise, title, their support base, and their subordinates at all times. They are born leaders. They have courage, aren't afraid to take risks, and unlike the Hustler, they have the patience that is required to build something from the ground up. They believe in standardizing their operation – something we will explain in the class later. And even if they don't write rules, policies and processes down, they train people in their organization into them *thoroughly*. They like to see a project completed before they move on, especially if they don't feel their organization is strong and capable enough to take on more responsibility.

"But there is a *serious* problem with the Gangster. They frequently have an enormous ego and they value status as much as they do money. They also have a value system that causes them to not always make distinctions between legal and illegal conduct. Where the Hustler might bend the rules a bit to get what they want, a Gangster has no qualms about hurdling right over that line. The Gangster believes that crime can be a viable source of money. As a result, their two major weaknesses are at times fatal. The ego and value system which make for good business at times, can earn the Gangster powerful enemies who, if they don't kill or imprison them, *put the Gangster out of business*. They simply don't distinguish between right and wrong or always make ethical decisions.

"The Entrepreneur, well, that's you I think, Michael. You are perceptive, receptive enough to criticism, yet strong-willed, and skilled enough of an arranger to create an organization to pursue what you perceive. The Entrepreneur is creative and a good decision-maker. They are the most highly motivated of all of the nine types of personalities and they are the eternal optimist, and it is those two qualities that can become weaknesses.

"The Entrepreneur for some reason either thinks everyone is like them or holds out hope that everyone will sooner or later be like them. They just can't imagine that there are people in the world that *aren't* like them. As a result the Entreprenuer can be easily deceived, not so much in the stage of perceiving the opportunity, but absolutely in the phase of creating the organization to pursue it. In this way, they can be the total opposite of the Gangster. What the Gangster has mastered through intuition, experience, and wisdom about human nature, the Entrepreneur seems almost totally ignorant of. The Entrepreneur is no fool to be sure, nor a push-over. But they struggle at putting people in the right place and in the right role, they struggle with understanding the nature of power in an organization and human motivation other than their own."

"Man, *who are you telling*, I can't figure this out for the life of me. One day everyone is 100% with this and making great decisions and volunteering to get it done. The next, they are sitting back waiting for me to pick up after them and carry the load myself," he lamented.

"But hold on," I interrupted, "Don't be too hard on yourself, let me finish getting through the types and I guarantee you this will empower you to understand how to get things going and keep them moving."

After I was sure Michael had not lost faith, I continued.

<<<<>>>>

"Now let's meet the Businessperson. This is our role model, Michael. This person does not have the entire package, by themselves. But they know how to put it together. They know how everything and everyone works and they seek to be effective with people and efficient with things.

The Businessperson knows when to call on a Hustler and how to use her or him. They can spot a Gangster a mile away and know the risks involved and how to do business with them if necessary. And they are former Entrepreneurs themselves so they know every step of the process from perceiving the opportunity to building the organization that successfully pursues it.

"The Businessperson is the Entrepreneur who has reached the final stage of creating an organization that no longer depends on their physical presence in order to operate. In other words, things can run in the business without them being around anymore. And that is what separates the Hustler and Entrepreneur from the Businessperson. The Businessperson knows that the highest level to reach is building something from the ground up completely so you can move on from the daily work and hardly look back.

"The Professional is very important, Michael. You can't have a Business without them. The Gangster and The Entrepreneur realize this. The Hustler doesn't care as much because they don't really build organizations. At the most, Hustlers will have Professionals in their network that they call upon when this or that needs to be done. The Professional is skilled at what they do. They are really the best at what they do, because they are highly educated and trained. They also are paid relatively well, or well enough, to do what they do. And *that* is the problem with them. They are not risk-takers. Out of all of the nine personalities they are the most tied to the current 'system', or what we call the status quo – the way things are.

"For a Professional to leave his or her job to do something else or *do for themselves*, it takes a disaster or a crisis. In other words, they must be laid off or fired before they find the motivation and courage to be an Entrepreneur. The Professional is the Entrepreneur's best and worst friend, depending upon *when* they encounter them. It is the Professional who tends to be the most difficult for the Entrepreneur to read because if the Professional's comfort, salary and future in 'the system' has been threatened enough, the Professional begins to speak the language and rhetoric of the Entrepreneur. When this happens the Entrepreneur thinks they have found a kind of soul mate and the perfect partner in business they have been looking for. But it is not to be. If the right circumstances materialize the Professional will leave the new venture to go back and take a job. Or, they will serve two masters – watering down the entrepreneurial venture while they desperately seek to find the security of 'the system' again. It always seems like an Entrepreneur is competing for the heart and mind of the Professional. Whatever can provide the security and salary the Professional desires – the entrepreneurial venture or 'the system' – will win the loyalty of this peculiar personality.

"The Engineer could be considered a Professional were it not for how easy it is to spot the difference. The Engineer, while highly trained and educated and receiving a salary from 'the system,' is not motivated by status or money. They care about nothing more than just doing the work. They love what they do, and do it for its own sake. And no matter how hard you try, they will not pull their nose away from the task until it is completed to *their satisfaction*. Their dedication is admirable and their focus critical at certain times. But they are individuals who are very sensitive and must be handled appropriately. And you have to be careful how you compensate them. Sometimes your approval and compliment, and the acknowledgement of the impact and influence they have on the business is more valuable to them than a bonus check. Don't place money over certain forms of appreciation and recognition that engineers crave. *Remember, sometimes their entire being is wrapped up in their work and if you criticize their work in the wrong way, you may accidentally offend or insult them.*

"Now, the Salesperson is the key to success my friend. And these are some special people – strange, even, because the word 'no' does not mean a damn thing to them. Rejection means nothing to them. In fact, some Salespersons eat up rejection like candy. It's like they find nutrition in rejection – like taking vitamins. For them it is a numbers game – the more people they contact and try to sell, the closer they are to making a sale. In a sense they are like Hustlers who have more discipline. Nothing can stop them but themselves. They are highly motivated internally and externally and they require very little supervision or guidance once you reach a clear understanding with them.

"However, there can be a few issues with them. They may not take too well to structure, and they can have big egos, so you have to watch how they work with others. In the mind of some Salespeople because they are directly able to show how their work brings in the money, they may not be willing to submit themselves or follow the guidance or direction of anyone but the Businessperson or Entrepreneur. A Professional and Engineer will have problems, often, earning a Salesperson's respect.

"Next, let me breakdown the characteristics of an Ideologue. This is a hard one to read. They are sincere and have beautiful hearts, usually. They practically always mean well. They see the Entrepreneur's vision, support it well before others, and they can speak into it a bit with a lot of faith. Nothing breaks their commitment to a powerful idea, cause or set of principles. Ideologues can be some of the best support to an Entrepreneur in the earliest and darkest hour of trying to get something off of the ground. Their moral support is always invaluable.

"Unfortunately, the Ideologue places words and talking a lot, or what we call rhetoric, over taking action. I'm not sure what it is exactly, but there is something in the mentality of the Ideologue that does not make for building or effective action. Don't get me wrong, Ideologues are not necessarily lazy, but they are surprisingly unable to make obvious adjustments. To them, being right in their mind matters more than being effective in reality. Ideologues are not pragmatic. What I mean by that is that they are not good at negotiation or any group activity that requires compromise or give-and-take. They can be hard to work with, because they take positions that are 'pure' more than realistic. But a skilled Entrepreneur and Businessperson knows that an Ideologue can keep the willpower, enthusiasm, and morale of an organization up, provide early seed capital, and that they make for great advisers at times because of their intellectual powers.

"The Coordinator is so important, Michael, so important. Without her or him you have no help of gluing together or cementing the parts of your organization in terms of persons and things. The Coordinator is more than a Professional. He or she has training and education usually, but these special persons also have a form of wisdom that comes only from interacting with people and having to make decisions in a wide variety of circumstances. Coordinators are made, not hired. They have to go through a set of experiences before they fulfill the title they are given when first employed.

"In addition to that, Coordinators in some respects are able to work in any environment. They can work comfortably in an entrepreneurial endeavor or 'the system'. Once they are on board they are committed, either way. The checks must arrive on time, however, and you need to treat them fairly or else their great value makes other people want them, and they frequently get job offers elsewhere.

"But there is one thing that is almost always in doubt with the Coordinator. You never know how ambitious they truly are. And this makes for a risky situation. Because the Coordinator is capable of running the business in your absence you have to be mindful that some Coordinators interpret this form of power improperly and might think that their status as Coordinator qualifies them as an Entrepreneur and even a Businessperson. If that is the case you may eventually have a coup on your hands. If not, if the Coordinator does not have unbridled ambition and truly understands that being a Coordinator is totally different than being an Entrepreneur or Businessperson, then in a

Coordinator you may have found the Most Valuable Person (MVP) of your organization."

There was silence, and then finally from Michael, "Wow, you read almost everything I am going through with my team without ever seeing us work outside of class. Wow, is all I can say."

I was relieved by his reaction, "Well, that is not true, in a way. I *have* seen you all in *my own* business organizations, and professional experience, as well as those of others. The patterns are unmistakable and these nine types of people are real and exist in experience after experience. You can't build a business properly without eventually coming into deep understanding of human nature and the personalities we have in society, the job market and the workplace," I stressed.

"Michael, what your experience is telling me is that we need to go over all of this as a class."

"Yeah, because I definitely can't explain this to my business partners like you did!" Michael said.

"Maybe not right now, but the reason I want us all to go over this as a group is because everyone will see themselves and what they need to do to improve or become more patient – not just with one another but with our own progress as individuals. It is not just everyone else who fits into these nine personality types, in some ways we all at times can resemble them in one way or another, you know?" I asked.

"That's true because when you were talking I was thinking about some mistakes I made too!" Michael nodded his head back and forth as he agreed.

"So, let me just wrap it up a bit with some additional thoughts, ok?" I politely suggested.

"Sure, go ahead," he replied with interest.

I concluded, "Now, there are a few things to always keep in mind about these nine types when building your organization. First, timing is everything when you meet, negotiate and work with these individuals. If a Professional comes to you interested in helping you start the business, search his or her motivation carefully. This is true with anyone, but especially those individuals who have a tendency to need security. It could be due to family needs, bills that have to be paid, or bad experiences with risk-taking in the past. But whatever it is, get to the bottom of it. Be up front if you feel this person is motivated more by money than by building something and a sense of accomplishment and unlimited reward. Maybe there is a way for you two to work out an honest arrangement where they get security as soon as possible, while you struggle for a longer period of time.

"In the case of the Gangster, of course you need to be careful, but never forget that a Gangster is only a Businessperson with, perhaps, an out of control ego, and value system that has no problem with illegal activity. So, remember the six sources of capital. Some Gangsters originally became that because other sources of capital were not available. That is usually why people first bet on crime as an entrepreneurial option. If they can be reformed in these two areas you have a great human asset on your team. A Gangster turned Coordinator or Entrepreneur is only days away from reaching Businessperson status. If they can resist the temptation to cut corners you have a leader like no other.

"Be sure that if your business requires an Engineer at an early stage that you think carefully about how to manage that person as the business grows. Engineers are great to get things off of the ground, because they require little compensation or supervision – which most Entrepreneurs can't afford or provide anyway. But as you grow, and more people are part of the team, the Engineer may have problems with reporting to anyone other than you. The Salesperson may have this problem, too.

"The Hustler can make one terrific Sales or Marketing Vice President, if you allow them some freedom, but *not too much*. Remember their tendency is MADD, so if you can allow the Hustler to become an *intrapreneur*, someone who has a lot of authority to create business opportunities and pursue them *inside* of the business, you might unleash something incredible in your organization. Also, Hustlers make great advisers due to their critical and creative thinking skills, so remember you can use them in a few roles beyond what they have direct control over. This allows them to not feel stifled in an organization. They can really help in negotiations and deal-making. They know how to handle themselves in settings like that. The key might be having a great Coordinator who knows when and where the Hustler needs creative room and discipline.

"As the Entrepreneur, it is up to you to identify these types in your existing organization or how to recruit and attract them, when and wherever needed. Some people usually find it to their advantage to find a Coordinator-type to serve as a Chief Operating Officer (COO) and not as a Chief Executive Officer (CEO) but perhaps you need an Engineer first, in order to get some things built. I can make an argument for any one of the other eight coming to your side first as part of the organization you create to pursue the opportunity you perceive.

"The last thing I want to show you is a fun way for you and your entire team to discuss all of this and see more deeply into what motivates each member of the business partnership. Come here and look at what's on my computer screen. Write down that web address: http://www.bls.gov/oco/ which takes you to the free online version of the United States Department of Labor "Occupational Outlook Handbook" (OOH). This book tells you, for hundreds of jobs:

- the training and education needed
- earnings
- expected job prospects
- what workers do on the job
- working conditions

"It is a magnificent reference tool in its own right but I want you to use it differently.

"This book, more than any other I know of, is like a window to the heart, mind, and soul of a person who is trying to find their talents, skills and interests and develop and pursue them. By simply reading this book, a person can imagine themselves in a variety of roles, noticing if they have qualities and a background that might make them a good fit in any particular area. By seeing what is possible, and what makes people good fits for certain jobs, anyone can become just like an economist in an instant, visualizing themselves working in any field, anywhere, anytime, anyplace.

"And all you have to do is pick it up and just start reading. Within minutes, a person who feels they aren't good at anything, bored by everything, or unmotivated to pursue a line of work, will begin to become interested not only in all of the fields available, how much money they attract, and what is needed to qualify; but they will also immediately begin to think of their own special talents, skills, and interests in relation to these fields.

"Some people see the word "occupational" and don't get why an entrepreneur would benefit from this book. But there are few books that I would recommend to an entrepreneur before the "Occupational Outlook Handbook", because it shows you where opportunities are opening and closing in the economy in various fields and industries. That is the first benefit.

"The second benefit is that by reading this book, you too, as an entrepreneur, can begin to line up your skills, talents and interests with certain occupations and the aptitudes that are described as being good fits for certain jobs. Although you may not see yourself as in a 'job,' you still, as an entrepreneur, have many functions that you must fulfill and reading the OOH can fine-tune your skill set and maybe steer you closer toward a field that lines you up even better with an opportunity.

"The third benefit is that by going through exercises using the OOH, with your partners and team, you can see maybe more clearly where the talents, skills, and interests place them in a particular industry. Perhaps where you first thought to place a person is not as good as somewhere else. Also, using the OOH allows you to get the feedback from your organization about where they think they are best qualified to work and help. Remember, they know better than you what they love doing and helping a person see their talent and the work that is right for them can help you and everyone else see what the best position in the company is, or role they should be playing in the business," I said, logging off of the computer to show Michael we were done so that he could begin to relax.

After several seconds of him pondering something, he leaned back and said, "What this has made me see is that the people around me are not going to give their all if they don't see themselves in what we are striving for and what they are already good at doing every day. If they can't relate their background and what makes them happy to their work and the goals of the business, we are always going to have problems with motivation and following through on what we tell each other we are going to do. Ms. Desai, what you are sharing also helps us deal with who is good at what. In a business we all may try to *get in* but that only works if we find a way to *fit in* with others. Doing it the way you are saying can help us end a lot of arguments."

It was clear he was becoming more confident.

I just beamed over his clarity and returned faith in what we were all trying to accomplish with this entrepreneurship course.

Michael had shown me the way to bring this all into the classroom and I could not wait to call Mrs. Jackson to tell her.

# Section 3: The Basics of Entrepreneurship

# Chapter 7: Think Big and Test Your Ideas

"The future belongs to those who believe in the beauty of their dreams."

- **Eleanor Roosevelt**

"Enjoy the little things, for one day you may look back and realize they were the big things."

- **Robert Brault**

After a week of working on the nine personality types and allowing the students to freely discuss their interpersonal relationships within their business teams, Mrs. Jackson felt the class had a firm foundation to go deeper into the basics of entrepreneurship. I sat in on the first of three classes devoted to the topic.

"Alright everyone," she began "I want to go back over something we discussed at the beginning of the year which will help you individually and as part of your groups. It deals with the difficulty in balancing the need to be very creative with the need to challenge your ideas, goals and plans. You all know what tension is right?"

"Yeah, that's what Miguel felt when he wanted to ask Anne out!" Anthony said, with a funny but inappropriate reference to our classroom's most obvious but unacknowledged affair of the heart.

"Not quite and that will be enough of that, Sir," Mrs. Jackson said, looking sternly at Anthony but not long enough to hide an emerging smile.

"The kind of tension I am referring to is what exists between what we call creative thinking and critical thinking. These aren't always the best two terms to describe what's going on but what we mean by those two labels are ways of seeing ourselves and the world we live in, and thinking about them in ways that help us invent, innovate, make decisions and plan. So today, in a way that may be different for us, we are going to *think about thinking*." Mrs. Jackson explained.

The look on the faces of some of the students made clear they did not grasp the concept fully but were intrigued by it and willing to be patient.

With her usual confidence, Mrs. Jackson continued, "I already know what you guys are thinking – *how do you think about thinking?* And *can we really learn how to think – isn't this something we are born with?* These are great questions and are not inappropriate. By raising them you are already thinking about thinking!

"This is why all of us 'grown-ups' have been encouraging you to remember what it was like when you were 5, 6, 7, and 8 and how easy it was for you to imagine things and even 'daydream.' You still do it but not in the same way. That was all a form of thinking and yes, you weren't taught how to do it by a teacher like me. It was, and still is, natural. But it's harder to do, as we get older it seems. And this can affect our ability to become successful entrepreneurs.

"The problem with thinking about problems, opportunities and ideas – or even coming up with them – is that we get away from our natural strengths at the same time that we aren't growing out of thinking habits that may serve us in one way but limit us in another.

"Take out the material we placed in the folders in front of you. I want you to read the paper headlined, 'Can We Really Learn To Think?' and the quote in bold from the chapter called, 'Learning to Think: The Challenges of Teaching Thinking' by Ron Ritchhart and David N. Perkins from *The*

*Cambridge Handbook of Thinking and Reasoning* edited by Keith J. Holyoak and Robert G. Morrison:

…sometimes our natural ways of making sense of the world actually stand in the way of more effective ways of thinking. For instance, our ability to focus attention can lead to narrowness of vision and insight. Our natural tendency to detect familiar patterns and classify the world can lock us into rigid patterns of action and trap us in the categories we invent. Relatedly, already developed understandings constitute systems of knowledge that are much more readily extended than displaced: We tend to dismiss or recast challenges rather than rethinking our understandings, which is a deep and general problem of learning. Our emotional responses to situations can easily override more deliberative thinking. The phenomenon of groupthink, in which the dominant views of the group are readily adopted by group members, can lead to limited processing and discernment of information. These are just a few thinking shortfalls suggesting that truly good thinking does not automatically develop in the natural course of events.

Even when our native tendencies do not lead us astray, they can usually benefit from development. The curiosity of the child for discovering and making sense of the world does not automatically [lead] into an intelligent curiosity for ideas, knowledge, and problem solving, for example. Our ability to see patterns and relationships forms the basis for inductive reasoning, but the latter requires a level of precision and articulation that must be learned. Our natural ability to make inferences becomes much more sophisticated through systematized processes of reasoning with evidence, weighing evidentiary sources, and drawing justifiable conclusions. Indeed, for most thinking abilities that might be considered naturally occurring, one can usually identify a more sophisticated form that such thinking might take with some deliberative nurturing. This type of thinking is what is often referred to as high-end thinking or critical or creative thinking. Such thinking extends beyond a natural processing of the world into the realm of deliberative thinking acts aimed at solving problems, making decisions and forming conclusions.

After allowing the class to read the material, Mrs. Jackson opened the floor to questions and group discussion. Sandra was first to raise a question, "So, this is saying that what we need to focus on is the kind of thinking that leads to 'solving problems, making decisions, and forming conclusions'?"

"For our purposes, yes Sandra. But there are other points connected to what we are doing. In light of this commentary on thinking, which indicates its ability to be 'learned', it might be useful, then, to think of critical and creative thinking as both innate or natural habits and as acquired skills which can have a great impact on how we perceive and interpret reality. Remember our definition of an entrepreneur as one who conceives or perceives an opportunity and builds an organization to pursue it, and these are important business skills," Mrs. Jackson responded, from her knowledge of the lesson plan's bullet points.

"But Mrs. Jackson, being an entrepreneur means we are being creators or innovators – that is what we have been dealing with right?" Peter chimed in, trying to get at something.

"Sure," Mrs. Jackson replied

"Then, I think what Sandy said and what this says here is really only about critical thinking," he replied.

"Why do you say that?" the teacher responded to her student – obviously curious, and anticipating an insight from one of the class' most interested members.

"Because perception of an opportunity has to come before those other business skills. You don't make final decisions when you are still coming up with a concept, right?"

Beaming with pride and an aura of amazement, Mrs. Jackson nodded her head, and gently said, "Yes, that's the tension we mentioned earlier. There can be a lot of tension in the relationship between creative and critical thinking because, in one sense, creative thinking is about being free and creating motion, while critical thinking can be about discipline and structure and order.

"Class, what Sandra and Peter are saying is very important so let's read some more on how thinking is learned, and the relationship between creative and critical thinking, to drive their points home.

"Look now at the material from *Becoming A Critical Thinker* by Vincent Ryan Ruggiero," Mrs Jackson said, guiding her students into an understanding more like a tour guide than a classroom instructor:

You are staring into space, imagining you are headed for the airport. You picture yourself ready for a month's cruise in the Caribbean, your pockets stuffed with cash. Would this mental process be thinking?

Now imagine you're discussing politics with friends. "It's always the same with politicians," you say. "They're full of promises until they're elected. Then they develop chronic amnesia. I can't see why people get excited over elections." Would you be thinking in this case?

Thinking…is purposeful mental activity. You control it, not vice versa. For the most part, thinking is a conscious activity. Yet the unconscious mind can continue working on a problem after conscious activity stops – for example, while you sleep.

Given this definition, your ruminations about a Caribbean cruise are not thinking but daydreaming, merely following the drift of your fantasies. On the other hand, your discussion of politics may or may not involve thinking. We can't be sure. You might not be thinking at all but just repeating something you'd said or heard before.

Thinking is sometimes regarded as two harmonious processes. One process is the production of ideas (creative thinking), accomplished by *widening* your focus and looking at many possibilities. The key to this process is to resist the temptation to settle for a few familiar ideas. The other process is the evaluation of ideas (critical thinking) accomplished by *narrowing* your focus, sorting out the ideas you've generated, and identifying the almost reasonable ones.

Both processes are natural activities for human beings, but we rarely perform them well without training and diligent practice.

"Now think of that in terms of the general definition of an entrepreneur as one who conceives or perceives an opportunity and creates or coordinates an organization to pursue it. We didn't invent it and it is not the only way to describe it but I think this general and easy to remember description of entrepreneurship works well in helping us see how this relates to our thinking," Mrs. Jackson said after reading the material herself.

"We learn primarily in four ways: conversation, observation, reading, and experience and many of us strengthen our willpower by three means – suggestion, visualization and prayer. Some categorize these last three as forms of meditation and consider it a fifth form of learning. One will find that in the lives of a great many successful entrepreneurs or businesspersons, these last three activities were what they credit with helping them develop ideas and persevere through difficulty, and remain confident in their ability to obtain the objective they sought after.

"One of the most inspiring examples in entrepreneurship and business is the story of the man who owned a couple of the hotels you have seen downtown or maybe even stayed in – Conrad Hitlon. He certainly read, observed, had many conversations and experiences, but he also practiced visualization, too. Richie, I want you to read from the page in the folder headlined "From 'How to Find a More Satisfying Career'" by Victor M. Parachin:

Legendary hotelier Conrad Hilton knew how to use this technique. The Great Depression was exceptionally hard for Mr. Hilton. After the stock market crash of 1929, people didn't travel as much, and when they did they didn't stay in the hotels Mr. Hilton had acquired during the roaring 1920s. Business at his hotels was so poor that by 1931 his creditors were threatening to foreclose. He was so financially destitute that even his laundry was in hock and he had to borrow money from a bellboy to eat. That year, Mr. Hilton came upon a photograph of the Waldorf Hotel. It had six kitchens, 200 cooks, 500 waiters, 2,000 rooms and a private hospital and railroad in the basement. He clipped the photograph out of the magazine and scribbled across it, 'The Greatest of Them All.'

'The year 1931 was a presumptuous, outrageous time to dream,' Mr. Hilton would later write. Nevertheless, he put the photo of the Waldorf in his wallet, and when he had a desk again, slipped the picture under the glass top. The magazine photo was always in front of him. As he worked his way back up and acquired new, larger desks, he would slip the cherished photo under the glass. In October 1949, 18 years later, Mr. Hilton bought the Waldorf.

Standing up and pulling out a page from *Sports Illustrated*, our class comedian, Terry, said, 'So, let me see, if I look at this dunk here by Dwayne Wade long enough, I'll do it eventually?' to a chorus of giggles.

"I think you know there's more to it than that, but the point, I think, of this story is that there was one constant in Conrad Hilton's entrepreneurial life – even when he was practically homeless – and that is the image and vision he desperately wanted to fulfill in life remained in front of him. He credits that as a factor in his determination." Mrs. Jackson said warmly but firmly.

'No, I know, I'm just playing – a lot of things can inspire you to keep going when people hate on you or say negative things. It's true," Terry reaffirmed.

"I'm glad you agree Terry," Mrs. Jackson said, with a smirk and smile. "Now let's go through the rest of the material in the folder because I want to be certain that you are grasping the relationship between being creative and being critical in a way that supports your business activity. I think it helps to boil everything down to four steps so that things are easy to remember. Keep in mind volition is just another word for will or willpower.

"Take out the material from Dr. Frank Channing Haddock and the excerpt we include from his book *Power of Will*:

We thus perceive four steps connected with the act of willing:

1) Presentation in mind of something that may be done;
2) Presentation in mind of motives or reasons relating to what may be done;
3) The rise in mind of Sufficient Reason;
4) Putting forth in mind of Volition corresponding to Sufficient Reason.

Mrs. Jackson then interpreted what the students were reviewing, "Here we can see that first the idea and image are created and described (visualized), then a reasoning or critical thinking process takes place, then the decision is supported by the will to move forward to the objective.

"I hope it is becoming clear that while creative and critical thinking are different, they are intertwined. Every single one of the great entrepreneurs I have read about who excelled at critical thinking, also practiced one, two, or all three of the following methods: prayer, affirmation, or visualization. They used some form of meditation or reflection to bring forth and develop an idea and then to become more determined in pursuing it or building a business around it. They did so whether or not they claimed a religious or spiritual faith, or belief system.

"I'll put it on the board now – the four steps that I see to bringing creative and critical thinking into entrepreneurship and business," Mrs. Jackson stated for the entire class.

**The Creative Thinking Process (Steps 1 and 2) involves the process of one being stimulated by something outside of them or producing a thought or idea from within (or both) – the perception of an opportunity, which is followed by an accompanying image and the visualization process, which gives that thought or idea greater structure and form.**

**The Critical Thinking Process (Step 3) involves the process of comparing and contrasting values and beliefs in relation to the perceived opportunity that has been visualized. Logic is used to make arguments that challenge and support the idea or image. This represents consensus-**

**building through an internal dialogue and debate, characterized by rational thinking and reasoning.**

**The Execution Process (Step 4) involves – in the event of a decision to move forward – determining to accomplish the goal; supporting and protecting the will to do so; planning, and creating an organization to pursue the opportunity to doing so (successfully launching business).**

"Even one of the most powerful statements made by the great writer on entrepreneurship and the power of the mind, Napoleon Hill – author of *Think and Grow Rich* – seems to embody this four-step process. He wrote [numbers inserted by this author], "Every human being who reaches the age of understanding of the purpose of money wishes for it. *Wishing* will not bring riches. But (1) *desiring* riches with a (2) state of mind that becomes an obsession, then (3) planning definite ways and means to acquire riches, and (4) backing those plans with persistence which *does not recognize failure*, will bring riches.""

"Now in closing I want to connect what we are learning today with our previous lesson on the nine personality types. One of the great things about being in a group of diverse people is that when you have a great big idea for a business or want to do something really creative, they can provide the internal debate and dialogue you need to form a consensus about how to pursue it. Some in your group are skeptical and others are more encouraging but you need both of these attitudes to really test a concept and see if it is worthwhile or has a chance to succeed. The more points of view in a circle of people who respect and trust one another, the better the creative and critical thinking that can take place. Unfortunately, too many of us get excited about an idea or a concept and try to execute it without subjecting it to healthy criticism.

"Sometimes the person most critical of your goals is a better friend to you than the person who won't ask you tough questions that make you think about what you are trying to do. Does that make sense?" Mrs. Jackson asked.

Within seconds, it seemed, the entire class was nodding their heads in unison.

Summarizing the point of this lesson quite well – for her own benefit as much as the class – was Melanie, a relatively quiet student, who said, "I've always been told that being a well-rounded person in high school mattered as much as anything else but because you don't get a grade in a class called 'Being Well-Rounded', it didn't seem to really matter. But to be a really good entrepreneur, it seems, all of the things and experiences you get from playing sports, or being in the marching band, or glee club, debate club or anything called extra-curricular, can help with creative and critical thinking and handling internal debate and stuff like that. It's like a real classroom outside of a classroom that you don't get a test score on until you leave school – where everything from daydreaming to arguing with one another can be good."

I was moved by Melanie's words and how well the class was going.

I gave Mrs. Jackson a thumbs-up from the doorway as I left, more convinced than ever that entrepreneurship can be a laboratory where every bit of learning and school experience can be applied.

*Thinking about thinking*, I like the sound of that.

# Chapter 8: Business Planning

"Planning is bringing the future into the present so that you can do something about it now"

**- Alan Lakein**

"I try to learn from the past, but I plan for the future by focusing exclusively on the present. That's where the fun is."

**- Donald Trump**

Today was the day.

I'd been working for months on getting the students access to some of the best business minds in the city, and we delivered: Rafael Stewart – managing director for the city's largest private equity fund – after working out a scheduling conflict, was coming in today for a guest lecture on business plan writing.

Anything involving an enormous amount of writing is usually intimidating – not only to high schoolers, but practically anyone.

Add to that the lack of familiarity with business and it was obvious to me that the subject of 'business plan' writing would have to be taught in a more interactive and supportive way than the usual lesson plan format.

So, after several meetings and outreach, the faculty agreed that Mr. Stewart – whose firm has overseen over $1 billion in investments to entrepreneurs, small businesses, and major corporations – had not only the knowledge but communication skills and personality that would engage the class.

Finally, he was here.

"I'm ready, no, *psyched*, Ami," he said after greeting me in my office 30 minutes ahead of class time to discuss what he was going to present.

Stylish frames, custom-tailored suit, and well-groomed, the 50-something investor was a walking example of much of what the class had been learning about business etiquette. I was impressed by his enthusiasm, too.

"What I want to do immediately is take the edge off of the fear these students have about writing business plans, and just as importantly, presenting them to folks like me, who have the power of life and death over their dreams," Mr. Stewart said with assurance.

"Mr. Stewart, thanks…" I started.

"Ami, please call me Rafael, and always that in front of the students, I feel old enough with each passing day!" he said with hearty laughter. "If they can't relate to me or feel comfortable, then I can't reach them with this, so even though I came dressed formally to fit in with your format, I'm going to communicate more casually, if that's OK."

"No problem at all, Rafael," I said with full understanding.

"For me the goal is getting them to see the business plan as practical and helpful and not a massive homework project which someone can reject. Believe it or not, most entrepreneurs that come to me for money have more anxiety over this part of the process and I think that is because the business plan represents the worst of two life experiences: homework assignments and public performance!" Rafael said with excitement.

I nodded my head, reclining a bit in my office chair, interested in where he was going with this.

"I mean, who wants to spend countless hours on a plan – doing research and writing – only to submit it to people very likely to reject what you have to offer without much interaction or engagement. I mean, we investors have an enormous amount of power in this process and I want to share and give that power back to the students and entrepreneurs, so that regardless of the outcome of what we call the 'capital raise', the experience empowers them and adds value to their continued planning, increasing their chances for success in the future. I *totally reject* the terrible tradition in the world of venture capital and private equity of people being devastated because someone said 'no' to them in response to a request for funding. Business planning is so much deeper than asking and receiving, or asking and not receiving!" he said with the kind of passion that convinced me this was as important a day for him as it was for the students.

"I'm sold, Rafael! Now let's go talk to the class – they're waiting for you," confident I had a presentation that would win with a sometimes skeptical audience.

He was so enthused he didn't realize I was bringing him in 15 minutes early.

<<<<>>>>

After taking the time to personally introduce himself and shake the hand of each student in the class, Rafael connected his mini-computer pad to our projector, took off his jacket and got into it.

"First, I'd like to tell you how honored I am to be with you all today. This opportunity has been so important to me that I literally changed my schedule around so that we could spend quality time together. I hope that when I leave today you will feel that including me in this wonderful course and process you are going through left you with something that will help you for your entire life," Rafael began, in a much more gentle tone than the one he spoke in earlier with me in my office.

"As you already know, we are scheduled to go over business planning and I want to share a few things with you about it but," Rafael paused as he looked back at the blackboard "But I want to do it in a way that is real so that you can feel me and relate to this as you work together in your business groups. So, I want to start by showing you I'm a student too, and I'm learning a lot from you and your teacher, Mrs. Jackson."

Rafael paused to nod to Mrs. Jackson who smiled back at him.

"So I did my homework and submitted it to Mrs. Jackson, a little late too!" Rafael said to a chorus of laughter from the class.

"And I got so much out of the last subject, dealing with creative and critical thinking."

As he spoke, my jaw almost dropped to the floor not realizing how much attention to detail our 'guest lecturer' had taken in our effort.

I was impressed beyond words.

"And what I got out of it was how important you all are to helping each other think through things. I want to stress that because *creative and critical thinking is business planning*," he said, looking at every member of the class, it felt like, to add effect.

"Can you all see that – anyone?" he asked, spontaneously engaging the class.

Sandra raised her hand.

"Yes, please tell me what you think," he said with a warm and inviting tone.

"Yeah, I wanted to know, since you read everything, what is the best way for us to test out the ideas we are looking to plan out, so that we don't waste time?" Sandra said delicately but in pursuit of something she was struggling to find.

Rafael was more than ready, "That's an awesome question young lady. Yeah, the way to start – if you have an idea – is you debate it with some good, trusted friends. You trust their integrity and their intelligence and then you debate. Once you start with some of your friends and somebody who knows something about your business and the idea passes that scrutiny then if you have access to a 'mentor', that would be the next step – engaging them about it. You need to speak to someone with some experience who can give you better feedback than what you received in the informal discussion with your friends. But every good idea starts with a good debate among a diverse group of people – and then someone with experience – whether in management, business, finance or starting up businesses or with knowledge of a product – just to give a broader picture and good debate going. If you succeed in convincing someone who is a good debater, I think that is a good start."

Seizing the moment, Terry raised his hand but found the perfect timing to politely ask a question without being called on. But our talented class comedian was serious, and there was no joke coming Rafael's way from him, "But how long should you keep an idea to yourself and work on it before you let other people know?" he asked, so innocently.

Rafael responded without hesitation "If you have a very good idea that you are afraid that others might steal from you, only discuss it with people that you really trust. In some businesses this is more important than others. If trust is present, when taken as a whole, these nine personality types you are learning about can create a balance that will protect and evolve good ideas, and destroy and discard bad ones. They are complimentary and if you can put an inner circle like this together you may be amazed at what they see in what you are doing that you – by yourself – can't see. The critical point I want you to get is that internal debate with a diverse group of people who don't necessarily agree with you is not just healthy, it is a *necessity*. Surrounding yourself with a bunch of 'yes-people,' who will never challenge your views, or surrounding yourself with critics who will never encourage a good thought is not good for you. We want to think together objectively and talk things out before we reach agreement or consensus with one another."

"Right, right, that's what we were talking about in class, thanks," Terry said in a contemplative mood.

With everyone fully engaged, our guest teacher continued, as if he were testifying, "Look, I know how you all feel. I still can't forget the first time I wrote a business plan. I spent a whole week, stayed up all night, for a 12-page plan that never got me a dime."

"And I have written and read so many plans since then – hundreds, if not thousands. I've been hired by multi-million dollar corporations to analyze their business plans and to help them raise money. And I have reviewed plans for friends, colleagues and family members who have been asked for investment or loans in business ventures," Mr. Stewart recounted to assure the class, although it was clear they didn't need it.

"So believe me, I know how annoying the process can be before, during, and after the plan is put together. But because of those experiences and my relationships with numerous consultants, advisers, economists, and my role as an investor, I can tell you some things that most entrepreneurs don't know about plans."

Sipping a bit of coffee, we placed on a desk for him, Rafael leaned forward with a question, "How long do you think a business plan has to be to get in front of a professional investor who has millions, even billions at their disposal?"

Peter weighed in, "That's easy. The software program and the reading I did all say that your plan should be flexible in size because different investors and banks want different information. But basically the finished examples that they show you are all like 15 to 30 pages long. I saw one plan that was 96-pages long! It looked like a book."

"Yeah, tell me all about it," Rafael said. "That is the common belief out there. But you go and talk to real serious investors or the person or people they hire to analyze business plans for them and you should walk away with a consensus, that 'less is more'. The smaller and more organized the initial plan, the better and more likely it is that it will be reviewed."

He then asked, "Guess how long the ideal initial business plan should be, from my experience and according to the experts I know and trust?"

"I don't know. Tell me," Peter said, with intrigue.

"No more than 3 pages," Mr. Stewart said calmly.

'*What?*' and '*No Way*' were the collective replies of at least 15 students.

"That's all. And now you are ready for another secret. Guess how long you will probably have to present the plan, and make a lasting first impression, to a top-of-the line investor?"

"1 to 2 minutes," he answered, not really waiting for a class reply.

"Now I know what you're thinking, so let me explain a bit," he requested.

"I'm not here to argue with what you have read or heard, or the business plan software you went out and bought or whatever you may have looked up on the Internet. But in the world of equity investment, which is where we want to be, more and more, as entrepreneurs, what I am telling you is real. Just think about it from the investor's perspective for a minute. If you, as an entrepreneur, don't want to write a 25-page business plan, who wants to read one? And not just one from you, but one from tens and hundreds of people who all want money at the same time. So, many of these investors only accept up front a brief business plan, and then, on top of that, if you have a chance to present it, they won't allow you more than 2 minutes to explain your business and make your case.

"I know this sounds exciting and troubling at the same time. On one hand you are thinking that it sounds like less work and a more efficient process. And on the other, you are considering that this makes for a harder mountain to climb. I can understand that. But what I think this information reveals is that only those folks who really know and believe in what they are doing are going to be that cream that rises to the top. Think about it. Imagine how thorough your mastery of what your business is about and what you are planning to do would have to be to organize it all in three pages or less, in writing, and 2 minutes or less in a verbal presentation. That is something to strive for, and it would signal to a potential investor that you are more likely to have thought through all sorts of things that can make your business succeed or grow."

"Yeah, yeah. I see your point," one of the students chimed in – I could not make out who was speaking from where I was sitting. "If I am not on point, why should someone give me money?" the male student finished.

Giving a thumbs-up, Rafael continued, "And here, you guys, is maybe the only real place where I strongly disagree with the traditional approach to business plan writing and what I feel is a dangerous misperception among entrepreneurs. You see, most people have the attitude that the main function of the business plan is that it serves as a 'trigger' to get you money. I strongly disagree and think this is dangerous for you to accept.

"No, I say. The business plan is a process that organizes you, *making you not a trigger, but a magnet that attracts* money. One of the worst things an entrepreneur can do is take the attitude that a business plan is something that can be written for them. That all they have to do is dump a bunch of paper on an 'expert' and that person will magically get you money by using words.

"It is not just what a business plan can *get for* you, as much as what it *does for* you that makes it so valuable. The business plan is what takes you from being an entrepreneur to a business man or woman. The business plan forces you to maximize your own creative and critical thinking ability. By relying on someone else to write it for you, you deprive yourself of the rich experience of gaining confidence, accuracy, persuasiveness, efficiency and effectiveness in what you propose to do, or are already doing.

"I would not trust a person with a start-up if I knew they had *not* been forced to think through the issues, questions and reality a good business plan writing process ensures. It would be like giving a talented teenager a million dollars. Without knowing exactly how the money will be used, you are setting yourself up for a problem that is potentially greater than the one million dollars.

"You talk to any serious investor or business plan analyst and they will tell you they want to know that an entrepreneur has done what we call the 'due diligence' or heavy lifting of business planning. That's just another way of saying, 'doing your homework' and knowing what you are talking about and trying to do. An entrepreneur who is not involved in a good thorough planning process is more likely to have the business get away from their control – growing too fast or too slow – and much more prone to mistakes and errors because they haven't, on their own, thought through opportunities and challenges. Not being involved in planning is also a good way to get robbed by dishonest partners, investors and employees."

Sandy agreed, "Right, being involved shows that the person is not just good at work, but will be good in business. I definitely think an entrepreneur should have thought more about what he or she is doing than anyone else – including a business plan expert or a potential investor. If I can see where they didn't do their homework, then I would not want to give them the money too."

"You see what this is about," Rafael said and continued, "There may be some bank or government agency that will give you the money for some reason other than your idea or good planning. Maybe they will give you the money because you have collateral – own a house or piece of property that is worth something and which they can get if you fail to pay back the money – or maybe because you qualify for a special program. But those reasons don't really deal with the business idea, plan, or team. And it is more likely that *all you will get* is money from them. When you step in front of an equity investor who is purely making a business investment and expects a return on that investment, you are dealing with a person who cares about your business – as an idea, plan, and team to execute it. If they give you money it is because they have confidence that things can work as you describe and that they will be there to help the business succeed, because it is in their own interests.

"So, at the end of the day, as an entrepreneur, you should want that test. I want to know that no one can ask me a question about my business that I or my team can't answer. I don't want a business plan expert knowing more about my business than me, because I am the entrepreneur and owner, not them. If I can meet the challenge of thinking through best and worst case scenarios, possible surprises, opportunities and how I want to grow, then I deserve to get money and I believe that confidence and a strong plan will help me attract it."

The class was ready, I could tell, and so could Mr. Stewart as he asked everyone to pull out the folder placed in front of each of them.

Before the students was everything they would need to write that initial business plan and help them make tight presentations in future networking opportunities and meetings seeking investments in front of a panel – which they would later experience as part of the course.

Here is what they saw:

## The Three Page Business Plan ™

### 3-Page BP

The 3-page business plan exercise is where creative thinking and critical thinking meet. It is designed to force you to answer certain questions about your existing business or idea; define it with clarity; and project its growth. The exercise develops the 'business model' and tests its chances for success. It also is the basis for a plan presented for consideration by an investor, and a much larger more thoroughly detailed business plan. By doing this exercise you lay a powerful foundation for the establishment, maintenance, and strategic growth of your business, or determine relatively quickly if you have an unworkable and non-viable idea or model.

Here is the outline – several sections and a brief description of what goes into each. Remember, all of the areas should be addressed *in a combined three pages*. This may seem difficult at first, but being concise and succinct will sharpen your thinking and aid in future presentations to investors. Of course a more detailed explanation and justification for what is written can be provided and included in a notes section, if you desire.

***

I.   **Founder's/Partners' Background**

From where have you come, personally, in the way of professional and entrepreneurial experience, that qualifies you (and your partners) to execute what you have in mind as a business? It should read like a resume in bio form. Not too wordy.

II.  **The Business Description**

What business are you in? What do you offer and to whom, broadly speaking? <u>Why would/do people buy or 'use' what you offer?</u> What need or want does your offering satisfy? What problem does it solve?

### III.  Competition, Substitutes, and Differentiation

From where is your competition most likely to come? What can 'substitute' for your offering (substitutes are those products and services in markets and businesses other than your own, which can serve the same function as what you offer, even if that is not their stated purpose)? How do you intend to remain aware of competition and 'substitutes' and their demand? <u>How will you make your offering appear different from your competition and substitutes</u>?

### IV.  The Most Profitable Demand Segment

Of those to whom you offer your product/service, categorize them into three to five different market segments (use any category you like – class, income, geography etc. or a mixture). Which market segment do you think is the most profitable, in terms of a return on your investment of time, resources and energy? Be clear about whether or not your most profitable market segment changes or is different over time. Is this segment loyal, and will they lead you to future business. How likely are they to refer you to others?

### V.  Your Organization

Other than the founders, who are the handful of leading people in your organization and on your team who will be helping you in the business? In one sentence write something of their qualifications and the position they will fill and role they will play.

### VI.  Operations Prototype

How do you produce and deliver your offering? <u>How would you standardize your business ('standardize' means setting up the business so that it does not depend upon your physical presence to operate)</u>? How long would it take to standardize?

### VII.  Marketing And Sales Prototype

How would you prospect, reach, and qualify potential customers and clients, then make the 'deal' or sale? In what order would you do so?

Are there certain clients and customers you desire whom you can get to right away and others that you would like to (or can only) reach 6 months, 1 year, 3 years and 5 years from now? What is the order of your sales and marketing campaign?

## VIII. Business Hierarchy and Infrastructure Expense

How much does your operations and marketing and sales prototype cost to set up and then maintain? How expensive is your infrastructure – team/staff, research, consultants, communications, supplied materials, customer service, place of business, and travel on an annual basis?

## IX. Revenue Projection

How much revenue – in dollar figures - do you project in year one? How much of year one's revenue – on a percentage basis – comes from your most profitable market segment? How much of year one's revenue – on a percentage basis – comes from other market segments?

## X. Valuation and the Ideal Investor

- Estimate your revenue over your first 3 years of business. Estimate your infrastructure expense over the same time period. By the end of Year 3 do you show a profit (in other words is your revenue greater than your expenses)? If so, take that profit and multiply it by 6. <u>That is a general projection of how much your business is worth today</u>. If you show $50,000 in profit in Year 3, the business is worth $300,000. An investor of $100,000 secures a 1/3 ownership stake.

- Think this process through and imagine the best type or ideal investment partner in your business, not just in terms of money, but also in terms of other resources they may bring to the table that can help you like management, experience, networks. How would you reach this ideal investor? What would be the investment in time and money?

- Should you take on an investor? Answer this question first in terms of these questions: Where do you want to be in three to five years in terms of profit and your most profitable demand segment? Can you get there on your own or with the partners you have now? Can you gain profit and revenue by giving up some ownership (remember 60% of $10 million is worth more than 100% of $3 million; but 40% of $2 million is worth less than 85% of $1 million )?

- What is the exit strategy? How does the investor get their money back?
- If you do not show a profit by your third or fifth year please consider that your idea and business model may not be viable.

<<<<>>>>

Rafael offered encouragement, "Now I know that some of this is new to you. Don't worry about that. There is a business glossary included in your course that defines these terms a bit more. But I do want to get into what standardization is all about next, when we talk about managing a business. But something else that is new to you and very important, that I want to look at right now, is the section dealing with what we call 'valuation'.

"To understand that, just look at the root of it, 'value'.

"We just want to focus on what a business is worth. I included an article for you to read and discuss which deals a little bit with why determining a value for your business is so important."

Rafael then asked everyone to pull that page out of the folder. Here is what the students saw:

In a section of his book *Where To Go When The Bank Says No* called, "Why You Must Value Your Business Before Talking To Investors", David R. Evanson writes (emphasis in bold is this author's):

"It's absolutely amazing," remarks John Lane, an investment banker in Westport, Connecticut, who specializes in emerging growth companies, **"how many companies looking for capital have not done any fundamental analysis to determine what their business is worth**, or are shopping deals with utterly ridiculous valuations."

You separate your deal from the pack with a well-conceived valuation analysis. It is important to have a clearly defined and well-delineated argument for your company's valuation, says Lane, because, except for those who specialize in one industry, "most equity investors have little concept of what a company is worth and need some guidance." The situation is analogous to consumers making big-ticket purchases. When there's a lot of money at stake, consumers carefully read product marketing literature to understand why the product costs as much as it does. Without this information many will simply move on to another brand.

In the same vein, without a valuation on the table, many equity investors – particularly high-strung and perennially overworked investment bankers – might not take discussions with an entrepreneur to the next step. It's not that they *can't*. There's just a greater likelihood that they *won't*. With raising capital so difficult to begin with, why make the task even harder?

**Entrepreneurs who look for equity capital without a valuation also give up the high ground and may surrender more equity than they have to.** "The advantage they lose," says Lane, "is that rather than *telling* the investor how much their company is worth and why, the entrepreneur ends up listening to the investor's assessment of how little their company is worth and why."

**The problem worsens when investors undertake the kind of analytical research that the entrepreneur should have done in the first place.** When doing this research, investors often develop a stubborn conviction about the value of the company. Therefore, know ahead of time what your company is worth and why.

Three basic points to keep in mind regarding valuation come from an article published in *Entrepreneur* Magazine written by Asheesh Advani called, "How to Value Your Startup". Mr. Advani writes:

**1. You are what the market says you are.** If investors are telling you that your startup is worth $1 million, then that's what it's worth. You might think it's worth more. You might even know it's worth more because your company may have more than $1 million in liquid assets, or more than $1 million in receivables, or more than $1 million in sweat equity. But if you're unable to raise money for your startup with a valuation above $1 million, then you'll have to accept the market valuation.

However, this isn't always true. If you raise money from relatives and friends rather than professional investors, it's possible that your company has been overvalued or undervalued (more likely, overvalued). For example, if you persuade your father and your rich aunt to purchase shares in your business at $20 per share, it doesn't mean that future investors will pay more than $20 per share–even if your business grows and prospers.

**2. But you can also tell the market what you're worth.** Although this might seem to contradict the point made above, it's possible to tell the market how to value your company. After all, if investors think your startup is worth $1 million, it's usually because of something you've told them. By definition, startups don't have a history of financial performance on which to base a valuation. Therefore, it's up to the entrepreneur to develop a process for valuing the company based on comparables and financial projections.

**3. You're not really worth anything until you're profitable.** If you're not profitable, your business probably isn't worth very much. That is, it doesn't have as much liquidity as it would have if it were profitable. Many businesses cannot be sold, since there aren't enough business buyers for every seller. Almost all unprofitable businesses cannot be sold for the same reason.

This makes valuation particularly challenging for a startup. Since young businesses take time to become profitable, the trick of valuing startups is to focus on the future. First, determine how many years it will take to be profitable. A business with a long road to profitability will usually be worth less than one with a quick path to profitability. Next, determine how much comparable companies have been valued at when they reached profitability. A company that could be worth $5 million at profitability will be worth some fraction of that number at the startup stage, based on factors such as the likelihood of success, the time frame to exit and the quality of the management team.

Rafael outlined all of this with the students for around 15 minutes and then said, "I know all of this you won't understand right away. But that is why I am here and you have teachers who will answer your questions on this in the future. I just wanted to be sure that I told you things others won't and gave you some information that you can refer back to as we finish the course and as you move on in life.

*"I'm telling you things most investors won't tell entrepreneurs.* So that makes me a snitch on your behalf, right?" The entire class broke out in laughter at Mr. Stewart's successful attempt at relating his points to something in the culture of the school and the community – people 'telling on others', for better or worse.

"But I *do* understand why valuation is important," Mark, a student who just moved here this year said, to the surprise of his classmates.

"You can hear about it in the music and movie industry and with sports teams. I just saw on the news a report on how much football teams were worth and I didn't know how much of their value came from things that had nothing to do with ticket sales to regular fans. I thought that was how they made the big money. But no, it is from things like TV contracts, selling jerseys, and endorsements from companies – a lot of different things that they add up to get a valuation before selling their whole team."

"You got it, man! And by keeping this stuff that I'm giving you today in mind, or at your fingertips, as entrepreneurs you can determine 'value' on your own terms and figure out who is the best source of money or the ideal investor from whom to get an investment or loan. Down the road you will do all of this not on your own, but with the help of financial experts like accountants, tax professionals, business appraisers and financial advisers, OK?"

The body language of the class expressed agreement and comfort with what they had just heard – enough for Mr. Stewart to continue, "Alright, we'll end on a couple of pointers," He said more like a promise than a statement.

He asked the students to grab from their open folders an excerpt from an article in the June 22, 2009 edition of the *Wall Street Journal*, called 'Why Business Plans Don't Deliver," and read it among themselves.

What they saw – from an inset in that article called "Telltale Terms" – was:

Many business plans fail to deliver because they cloud the opportunity in a fog of terms that make investors wince. Here are some words and phrases to avoid.

**Huge** (as in "Our market is huge!") Translation: The writer hasn't bothered to get reliable data on market size, or has failed to think carefully about the initial target market, which almost always should be quite narrow. Nike's initial target market of elite distance runners was minuscule, but it provided a solid foundation for growth.

**Conservative** (as in "We conservatively forecast that…") Investors know that the initial sales numbers—never mind the profits—rarely pan out. So, let the numbers speak for themselves, based on the evidence you've gathered.

**Revolutionary** (as in "Our revolutionary technology…") Translation: "We are so enamored with our idea that we have not thought clearly about how to distinguish it from other approaches and are not interested in what the customer thinks of it. Customers simply aren't visionary enough to fully appreciate our technology…."

**Assumptions** (as in "Assumptions for the figures in our financial statements") If you are "assuming" most of your numbers, you'd better stop now. A far better notion is "Evidence that underlies each of the figures," set forth in a table in front of the financial section so the figures can be readily used to stress test the plan in advance as well as to update the plan as further evidence becomes available.

**We believe** (as in "We believe that…") Translation: "We haven't bothered to obtain a shred of real evidence, because we've been too busy writing this business plan to actually gather any evidence, but it is our desperate hope that…" If you don't have any evidence, stop writing and go get it!

**No competition** (as in "We have no competition.") If there's a single phrase that can send a business plan directly into the trash, this is it. Of course you have competition! They just haven't heard of you yet. To prospective investors, perhaps surprisingly, competition may be a good sign, as it suggests that there's a problem that someone besides you thinks is worth solving.

"I can tell you are ready now for me to get into something else that is so important," Rafael said with a slight accent I could not identify. Maybe from Spain, I thought.

"If there is nothing else that I want you to leave this course with today – and I hate to say it that way because all of it matters – it is that I want you to be super clear on why most businesses fail. You gotta' know the biggest blunder small business owners make, over and over again, like a broken record."

With nearly 40 young adults hanging on his every word, the discussion now went in a new direction.

# Chapter 9: Management and Execution

"All great achievements require time."

- **Maya Angelou**

"When you do the common things in life in an uncommon way, you will command the attention of the world."

- **George Washington Carver**

"Of the nine personality types this class has discussed," Rafael stated, "the one that I want you to focus on now is that of the Coordinator. That is the role most closely related to management and execution and the subject of why so many entrepreneurs and businesses fail before they get started.

"I found one of the very best descriptions of what management is in a book, *The History of Management Thought* by Claude S. George, Jr. He wrote, "Managers create an environment conducive to the performance of acts by other individuals (1) to accomplish a collective objective or goal, commonly called the firm's goal, and (2) to achieve one or more of the goals of the participating individuals. *Determining the collective objectives of an undertaking and generating an environment for their achievement is the total function of a manager.*"

"That's the same thing, basically, as the Coordinator you all have been studying. That's their role – making sure things are in working order and working toward the objective.

"And with that said we can get straight to the point: most businesses fail because the entrepreneur who starts them lacks management or execution skills, or when to use them. They have trouble playing the role of Coordinator and, as a result, the business ends up not growing beyond their own involvement. The secret to success is building a business in a way that it does not always depend upon any one person to do everything. That is called standardization. And all standardization requires excellent management and coordination.

"Years ago a good friend of mine reviewed a business plan I had written for a new venture I had in mind. I was surprised at his response. Although he did not deny the monetary projections or viability of what I had in mind, he said, 'You don't have a business here.' We went back and forth over this as he struggled to find words I would understand to make it clear that I had *something* that might make money but *whatever* it was, it was not a 'business'.

"We were not making much progress.

"Finally, a few days passed and I picked up a copy of a book – *The E-Myth Revisited* by Michael Gerber.

"The subtitle was: *why most small businesses fail.* That got my attention. The book had identified some of the key problems that cripple businesses. I read it, coming across a section where Mr. Gerber explains how valuable a contribution McDonald's has made to the world of business in how it has systematically standardized every aspect of its operation – from the way a hamburger is made, to the way the uniforms look, to the way the drive-through window runs. He spoke about it in terms of a revolution. He called it 'The Turn Key Revolution'.

"The fundamental insight Mr. Gerber repeatedly stressed was that *the way the business works is as important as the product or service it offers.* The way the business is formatted is the key to its success and value, which depends upon its ability to produce consistent results even when those working in the business are not very skilled.

"I immediately saw how this applied to my business plan. I wrote the business plan around practices, personalities and products but not around the business itself. So the business itself was not the central of the initial plan.

*"Then* I came across this tremendous insight in what I was reading: *if your business depends upon you, then it isn't a business.*

"I shared this with my friend, and he said that was exactly what he meant by his insistence that the business I proposed was not 'standardized'. He said that when a business depends upon a particular person to a great degree, quite often one will find that they will not be able to get forms of insurance for it. Insurers know that what they are being asked to back is not an organization that can run on its own, but rather one that depends upon particular personalities. In that case they would almost rather write a life insurance policy for you than one that covers your business.

"Now, please don't misunderstand. This does not mean that people are unimportant or that your business is not one until it is 'automated'. Without people you don't have a business either. But what Michael Gerber and my friend made clear to me is that without a format or prototype that does not depend on you, there is no independent business.

"If you are doing all of the work – you really have a *practice*, not a business. Most investors are less likely to invest in a 'business' that depends upon an individual more than it depends upon an organizational and operational system. They want consistent, reliable results that can be produced by individuals of varying skill levels.

"This is especially important for those investors who are looking for businesses that can obtain scale – grow to reach a certain level of operational size, revenue and market share. This might be the difference between a barbershop with 10 locations that is so standardized that every shop works the same and produces the same result for clients *and* a barbershop with one location that depends upon the physical presence of one excellent barber to attract clientele.

"If an investor has $250,000 to pour into a venture and wants to see the most return on the investment with the least amount of risk, it is more likely that they will invest in the *business that has a system in place that replicates and duplicates results* rather than one with no real system, that depends excessively upon one talented person, in one location. If that talented person gets sick then what?" Rafael asked.

"Then the business is a wrap!" Terry summarized, to the laughter of everyone, including our guest speaker.

Rafael agreed, "Right, this reality touches on why some entrepreneurs don't access capital from certain types of investors. The problem in this case is not that they are the wrong skin color, gender, or age in the eyes of the potential investors, but rather that the business they have established – because it relies on one or a few talented and skilled individuals more than an organized process – is seen as too small in terms of scale and potential. Because the business does not prioritize a systematic approach to specialization and a division of labor, it will never become big enough to attract certain levels of investment.

"Standardization is almost a secret – almost every investor knows how important it can be, while the exact opposite is true of young entrepreneurs who are unaware of it.

"Most entrepreneurs have never been taught how to build a business so that its production and operational processes no longer depend upon them, as an individual.

"I cannot tell you how hilarious it was for me to see myself in clear violation of this principle as an entrepreneur and how really enlightening and liberating it was when I became aware of what was happening. Knowledge is power, as Mrs. Jackson is teaching you every day. To better understand this, it helps to get acquainted with two concepts that you probably have different levels of familiarity with – systems theory and franchising. How many of you know about systems theory?" Rafael asked.

Only two students raised their hands.

"Now, how many of you know about a franchise business?" he followed-up, with 20 students raising their arms, high, in reaction.

Rafael smiled and said, "That's what I thought. Have you ever thought about what makes it so easy for so many people to get a job at a fast food restaurant? Just think about it.

"OK, I want you take out the next sheet in the folder, it should be a statement from Michael Gerber. It's from an interview he gave years ago where he talks about both systems theory and franchising."

Here is what the students saw:

**Michael E. Gerber:** Yes…When I was in Silicon Valley a consultant-friend of mine asked me to do him a favor, to consult, and I knew that I did not know anything about business. I had the assumption that business owners knew something about business; otherwise, why would they own one? The very first thing that I discovered about my assumption – that I didn't know anything about business – wasn't true. And my assumption – that people with businesses did know something about business – wasn't true. *I did know something that they didn't.* That basic thing that I knew, based upon experiences in my early life when I learned how to sell encyclopedias, is that *selling is a system.* That led me to see that none of the people I was calling on or working with who owned small businesses in Silicon Valley understood that selling is a system – there is a very specific way to do it.

Well if there is a specific way to do that *then there had to be a specific way to do everything.*

Being a systems thinker came as the result of my very real world experience using soft systems in order to be very effective at whatever I did. And those soft systems could be the way I learn to sell; learned to play the saxophone; learned to build a house with my own hands; learned to do anything that I needed to learn how to do.

I began to see that in fact all that I was understanding was that these were all systems.

The system by which one learns to be a saxophone player. The system by which one learns to build a house. The system by which one learns to sell. Now understand that playing a saxophone, building a house, and selling a set of encyclopedias are all obviously different things, and one could conclude that they are very unique. But I could see that these things *were not unique*. In fact, I could see the similarities in them all.

I understood that truly what is missing in most businesses are people who understand the relationship between all of these component parts of our lives which are systems. And a system is nothing more or less than a particular way of doing something, anything, and that can be identified.

If in fact that can be identified, that can be documented. And if in fact that can be documented, then it can be communicated. And if in fact that can be communicated, then that can be taught. And if in fact that can be taught, then it can be learned. And if in fact that can be learned, then it can become a skill. So, a system can be a skill. And if you have a skill, based upon a system, then, in effect, you can in fact teach anybody anything, where there is willingness and an interest in learning it. And if that is true, you can build a profoundly effective company based upon these words – "systems thinking".

Systems thinking is a very practical, real and obviously replicable way of relating to the world.

Every great company you look at has a very specific way of doing what they do – this is how we do it and this is who we are. Everybody else has created a business that is dependent upon great people.

So, if in fact you can define a great system, you can accomplish any specific task or result that you wish to accomplish. It means that you put that great system into the hands of a less extraordinary person – call them an ordinary person – and through that system, produce an extraordinary result.

Well if that is true, and of course it is – and you can find examples of that everywhere you look – then imagine the power of that in creating a business.

So, if one looks at the business as a product of the entrepreneur - the business is the product – then essentially the entrepreneur goes to work to envision a company that works better than any other company in whatever market he or she wishes to focus their attention on. And ultimately that company will end up being a completely-integrated system that produces the result that the entrepreneur envisions as necessary. *"When you absolutely, positively got to get it there overnight – call Federal Express"* – that's a system!

*Unfortunately, few companies have ever been built systemically.*

That's the opportunity – to teach people the power of systems-thinking, and the application of it, in the most ordinary and extraordinary things that we do. In the process of that you transform people's understanding of the world and the way it works. And in the process of transforming people's understanding of the way the world works, you actually can transform everything they do. And to the degree you can do that, you can truly have a profound impact on the economic reality that they find themselves in.

And that is the only way it can be done.

Change the way people *think* and you will change the way people *do*.

Continue to try to change what they do or to give them money to start businesses they haven't got a clue what to do with, and witness the same old results going round and round and round.

So unfortunately, from my perspective most economic development initiatives are doomed to fail because rather than changing people's thought process they try to change what they do. And you can't change the results of what people do by changing what they do – you have to change the way they think about it.

Change the way they think about it and everything is transformed.

**Question:** I want to isolate this because this goes deeper into a very illuminating part of your book. This whole concept of standardization and the franchise prototype versus the personality-driven enterprise that can be very lucrative but does not have permanence. Could you elaborate on this?

**Michael E. Gerber**: Well absolutely! The *prototype or metaphor* of the franchise – because I am not really saying that you should go out go and franchise your business. No, what I am saying is that you should *act as though* you are going to franchise your business.

So understand the "Business Format Franchise" and use McDonald's as the exemplar of this way of thinking. And please understand that I am not using McDonald's as an exemplar of anything else. I am only using McDonald's as the example of this way of thinking and the profound impact and scalability that is present when one thinks this way. McDonald's is in fact a *success-system*.

It was created by Ray Kroc, who was 52-years old at the time.

He created this "turn-key" operating system that had really already been pre-created for him by the McDonald brothers.

He first went to sell them a milkshake machine, and came away with the franchise rights to McDonald's. The franchise rights to McDonald's was his vision. In essence, he saw he could "turn-key" this thing, this hamburger stand operation (in San Bernardino, California) – even get it better than the McDonald brothers did it, and he thought he could replicate it tens of thousands of times.

So Ray Kroc went to work on McDonald's to build a franchise prototype – a perfect little operating system that Ray Kroc called the most successful small business in the world. And in the process of going to work on that business to create the most successful small business in the world, he built something that could be run by kids, at minimum wage, with a 300 percent annual personnel turnover – creating "the impossible" in an ordinary business – a hamburger stand.

He was able to create a multi-multi-billion dollar enterprise, and a way that anybody could do exactly the same thing. The idea and approach had potential because there was a market for it. It could differentiate itself from every other business by the way it does business and by the way it packages the system through which it delivers its promise to the customer.

Anybody, anybody, anybody can do what Ray Kroc did.

Anybody can build their own version of McDonald's, and they can do that not only in an ordinary business like a hamburger stand, but they can also do that in a business like orthodontics. They can do it in laser surgery, as in fact has been done.

But the important development is the turn-key process. By developing a turn-key operation, McDonald's can do in its thousands of stores what most of us can't do in one!

**Question:** Do you make a distinction between the standardized system as a business, and a person around whom a whole business revolves?

**Michael E. Gerber:** If your business depends upon you, you don't own a business, you have a job!

And understand that I am saying that it may be the most enjoyable job in the world and it may pay well, but ultimately it is doomed to fail. Now, *most* businesses are doomed to fail.

But ultimately *that* kind is doomed to fail – as soon as you do. So in other words, if your business is completely dependent upon you, that is, you have to get up every day to do it or it doesn't get done; that is not going to last past your ability or desire to wake up in the morning.

<<<<>>>>

After having each student read a portion of this interview, Rafael opened the floor to questions.

A student named Alicia said, "I've worked like three jobs in fast food and they showed us how to do everything in training. The manager told me that if we had any questions about what to do in any situation that he couldn't answer, the whole system had failed. They even have a university where he told me he had to go in order to learn all of the things he was using to train us. There were manuals, books, notebooks and everything that we use here. Every year he has to get trained again in new things, and *he's a manager at a place that sells fried chicken!*"

"What is your name?" he asked with excitement, looking to acknowledge her point and drive it home even further.

"Alicia is 100% correct in saying, '…questions about any situation…' That is what you have to think about when planning your business. Think together – creatively and critically – and imagine problems and opportunities that will arise in the life of the business. Think about how you would have to prepare the staff through training and information to deal with different situations. Include this in your budget – training and research.

"I know that your businesses – as part of this course – aren't being set up to last that long, but one of the things I would be looking for as an investor is that you have designed the start-up in a way so that it could eventually operate on its own under the coordination of a great management team who can execute your plans. So focus on those areas of your business plan because it is not just a great idea, product or service that makes you successful; it is how you plan and execute around it. And to do that you need good people who know how to get things done and coordinate activity.

"Two business leaders wrote a book about a lot of this several years ago, called *Execution: The Discipline of Getting Things Done.* One of the main points they make is that every business and the persons leading it has to deal with three things: people, strategy, and operations. Being more specific they write, "The leader must be in charge of getting things done by…picking other leaders, setting the strategic direction, and conducting operations. These actions are the substance of execution…"

"So, class, this won't be the last you see of me, but I want to leave you with some encouragement.

"No matter what event, business, or personality you see as successful, know that there is some process and level of management and definitely execution associated with what you are seeing, that is unseen.

"From a dinner at a fancy restaurant, to the delivery of your mail, to things like how a sports team is run or a song is recorded and marketed; there are lesser known people – as managers and coordinators – playing very important roles. If you are going to be a successful person in business you are going to have to see the process in three dimensions: 1) how business ideas are formed and products and services created 2) how business operations are organized, coordinated and managed and 3) in terms of the thinking, behavior, and experience of the customer whose business you desire.

"This course and your hard work will more than have you ready to do so," Rafael ended his formal presentation with us before joining the students and teachers for a catered lunch and informal discussion.

While I and Mrs. Jackson certainly appreciated his endorsement of our course, Rafael actually did not realize that only he could have added what he did *to* the course – an individual with real world experience in the challenging world of business, with final say over what ideas are funded and which are not.

No textbook, by itself, can or could provide that perspective.

And because he was able to deliver his message with passion and respect for the students, themselves, we all benefited.

I think Rafael, in some ways did too, more than faculty and students.

# Section 4: What No 'School' Can Teach You

# Chapter 10: Pain and Suffering is Good: The Price of Success

"You never find yourself until you face the truth."

**- Pearl Bailey**

"Adversity introduces a man to himself."

**- Unknown**

For years I have wrestled with something that I did not know how to address properly in public or with students. I am always so pleased to hear of any effort that promotes entrepreneurship, not only for young people, but anyone, anywhere. But over the years I have noticed how the subject of entrepreneurship in its most popular expression is usually always shown as an encouraging, optimistic, and positive activity – and it certainly is.

But that is not the whole story.

The history of entrepreneurship and creativity is always accompanied by pain and suffering.

The lives of the greatest inventors, and businesspersons show that their greatest creativity is accompanied by some of the most difficult circumstances people have lived through, in fact, it seems the difficulty in some ways encourages creative acts or a decision to take a risk or chance on a new idea, in business and in life.

I have felt then, that people in some way have not been telling the whole story of entrepreneurship because a less pleasant side exists to it, which may not attract people or which may disturb them.

I guess that makes sense – it is contrary to much of our thinking to see loss, shock, pain, and rejection as a form of positive fuel, or experiences which enlighten and guide a path to success and fulfillment.

However, the facts indicate that 'contrarian viewpoint' is reality and even the norm of the entrepreneurial experience.

But finally, one day, I found a way to introduce this dynamic in discussion.

That moment arrived when I learned about the 'unknown' side of the life of the great personal success author, Napoleon Hill.

Although over 20 million people have purchased Napoleon Hill's *Think and Grow Rich* – arguably the most influential book impacting entrepreneurs published in the last 100 years – it just may be that the book about *his* own life and writings, *A Lifetime Of Riches,* is even more important for one to read.

That claim may be strange, especially when one considers the reality that of all of the persons I know who have read or heard of *Think and Grow Rich,* only one has ever mentioned to me the book about its author which details the *excruciating* circumstances which preceded and surrounded the writing of *Think and Grow Rich.*

In other words, while millions and millions sing the praises of that famous little book, *Think and Grow Rich*, almost all of them are possibly unaware of the life and process that went into producing it.

That cannot be an accident.

There must be something in the story that people don't feel comfortable about, or which makes them so uneasy they don't share or promote it.

If properly understood, though, Napoleon Hill's life is not a tragedy, but an informative inspiration and instructive example – maybe more sobering and realistic than any other – of what an entrepreneur must go through in order to achieve success: a period, or extended periods, of suffering and adversity, a path that very likely causes pain in the lives of others, often unintentionally.

The inside flap of the book, *A Lifetime of Riches,* states, "Despite his connections with many rich and powerful people, Hill's personal life was a financial and emotional roller coaster. He watched his fortunes come and go as business enemies, world wars, a gold-digging second wife, and even the mob stole away his opportunities for wealth. Yet even when he was abandoned by his family, this incurable optimist and entrepreneur believed that every failure held a lesson for success."

How difficult was life for Napoleon Hill? What kind of trials and tribulations did his life represent to that of others?

Well, according to *A Lifetime of Riches*, Napoleon Hill:

- Was falsely accused of fathering a child at age 15 and deceived into marrying a woman under that pretense (The marriage was later annulled)

- Lost his job at a lumberyard when the yard went under as a result of the economic chaos produced by the Panic of 1907.

- Agreed to a book project at the age of 26 that would take twenty years to research and write without any compensation and no expenses paid except in the early stages. All in his family believed he had made a fool-hardy decision (The 20-year book project would become *Think and Grow Rich*). In giving him the vision and mission for the book, Andrew Carnegie told him, "The job will require twenty years, which during which time you must be willing to starve rather than quit."

- Married his wife, Florence, secretly, because he had no money and did not want to face the objections of his wife's parents.

- Had his automobile company taken over by a bank that had extended him credit for a business venture. Lost as well, at this time, was $4,000 of his wife's money which was placed in the business at the last minute

- On November 11, 1912, Napoleon and Florence's second son, Blair, was born, not only deaf, but without ears.

- When Blair was still an infant, and the Hills' first child, James, only a year and a half old, Napoleon left his family in Lumberport, West Virginia and headed for Chicago because he wanted to be someplace that would challenge him, and because he felt he was not doing whatever he was born to do.

- In 1915, his three business partners in the Betsy Ross Candy Store removed him from the company, had him arrested, and then blackmailed him for his interest in the company. He was vindicated but left flat broke.

- His wife had to borrow so much money from her family and carry so much of the financial and emotional burden of providing for the family and helping Napoleon Hill that her parents began to think that Napoleon was conning their daughter, his wife.

- In 1917, again with a loan from his wife, Napoleon gave the hardest year's work he ever performed to establish his first entrepreneurial effort in teaching success principles and salesmanship through his George Washington Institute.

- In 1918, the second military draft associated with World War I practically destroyed his school, taking away most of his students in the George Washington Institute, costing him $75,000 in tuition fees.

- With the birth of their third child, and Napoleon unable to provide for his family, nor himself, Napoleon's father, James, began to think that Napoleon was taking advantage of the goodwill and generosity of his in-laws – Florence's parents. The relationship between Napoleon and his father became more estranged as a result.

- On November 11, 1918, Napoleon Hill started a magazine, *Hill's Golden Rule* but because he had no funds to employ outside writers he had to write and edit nearly every word of the first nine issues himself.

- In October of 1920 Napoleon loses control of *Hill's Golden Rule* to his publisher, George Williams, largely as a result of a slanderous mud-slinging campaign led by a competitor and Napoleon's own secretary and associate editor. Napoleon is paralyzed for a month by grief, self-doubt and self-pity.

- In April of 1921 Napoleon Hill started his second magazine, *Napoleon Hill's Magazine*, having obtained seed capital from friends. Later that year, Florence became sick but because communication with Napoleon was so poor and she was so used to struggling by herself with financial and family problems, she did not mention it to Napoleon. But, as *A Lifetime of Riches* describes, "While Napoleon's domestic life began to erode, his career entered 1922 with more momentum than ever before."

- In late 1923, after establishing a successful prisoner reform program and organization, two of Napoleon Hill's directors in the organization engaged in corruption with the resources of the business. To make matters worse, they conspired with an old and envious nemesis of Napoleon's. Together they attacked him in the media with allegations and hired 'thugs' to disrupt Napoleon Hill's public lectures, challenging his integrity before crowds and clients. The campaign cut subscribers, newsstand sales and advertising in *Napoleon Hill's Magazine*. But most devastating of all, the old nemesis was able to buy the mortgage of the printer of the magazine and when Napoleon failed to make payments, his envious enemy foreclosed and stopped publication of the magazine. To add insult to injury, he was even successful in getting Napoleon investigated for mail fraud by the U.S. Postal Service. Napoleon was exonerated but had lost everything.

- Immediately thereafter, the building in which Napoleon stored his valuables in Chicago burned down. According to his biography, "Gone were dozens of letters and notes from Woodrow Wilson, including his approval of a Hill proposal that the president used to sell war bonds. Gone were the autographed pictures of Wilson, Bell, and others. Gone was President Taft's letter endorsing Hill for employment. Gone was a series of letters from Manuel L. Quezon, who corresponded with Hill prior to becoming president of the Philippine Commonwealth. And most devastating of all, gone were Hill's bulging files of confidential questionnaires completed by such luminaries as Luther Burbank, Thomas Edison, and hundreds more who participated in his research on the philosophy of success." Of these documents – gone forever – Napoleon Hill expressed his sorrow, "The loss of my magazine cost all of the money I had…my confidence in men had been terribly shaken…but those losses were nothing compared to the destruction of things that could never be restored; things associated with the memories of men who had been my greatest benefactors at a time in my life when their recognition was about the only real asset I possessed."

- Borrowing $1,000, Napoleon headed to Ohio and took over the Metropolitan Business College in Ohio. As with any start-up, money was slow and scarce and had to be put back into the business. But now his relationship with his wife and children, under this added strain, reached a crisis level. And emotionally in the winter of 1925, Napoleon reached an excruciatingly painful low, knowing that his suffering wife had lost confidence in him. In a letter to her he wrote, "You have no idea what it is like when not a soul on earth encourages you, and all the negative forces pour in on you. It takes superhuman strength of will to throw them off. I would give anything if I had someone, even though they did not mean it or believe it, to tell me they KNEW I COULD SUCCEED."

- When business picked up a bit over the next few months, Florence's spirits improved a bit, as did Napoleon's. In a poignant July 13, 1925 communication, Napoleon Hill wrote his wife a deeply introspective letter, acknowledging to himself what perhaps she already knew, of the paradoxical nature of his life and mission. Pointing to themes that the entrepreneur, inspired preacher and leader can relate to, Napoleon Hill wrote: "I have stood by the Law of Success lecture and my 15 points for more than seven years. At times they only seemed to mock me, when I was talking of success to others while my own family suffered for necessities. I have not known just why I did this. At times I wondered, as you have done, if I would not have been better off to have forgotten it all and have gone back to some little job as a bookkeeper, where I could have earned at least a modest living. BUT there was something that would not let me do it...I have stood my ground, suffered, been disappointed, and given disappointment to others all because I could not do otherwise. I was simply helpless in the matter...I would have changed my course a dozen times in the past six or seven years IF I COULD HAVE DONE SO."

- In early 1926, Hill struck up a relationship with *Canton Hill Daily News* publisher Don Mellet. Mr. Mellet put together a plan to finance an 8-book success series of Napoleon Hill's. But after he exposed a bootlegging operation that targeted children, in his newspaper, and obtained a commitment from Elbert H. Gary, Chairman of U.S. Steel to pre order $150,000 worth of the new book series, Mr. Mellet was murdered at home by a gangster and renegade police officer. Napoleon Hill returned home, learned of the news, and received an anonymous call telling him he had 1 hour to get out of town. *A Lifetime of Riches* describes what happened next, "Realizing the situation was hopeless, Hill left immediately, not even pausing to pack. Once more, he had struggled and scratched to follow the course of a rainbow. Once more, he had come within an arm's length of the promised pot of gold. And once more, it had been snatched from him just as he reached to touch it. Napoleon Hill would spend the forty-third year of his life in hiding in West Virginia, destitute, unable to support his stunned family, unwilling to go out of doors without a pistol in his pocket. For the first time in his life, he experienced the pain of constant fear.

- Even after the murderers of Don Mellet, who were after Napoleon Hill, received life sentences, the writer extraordinaire could not bring himself out of hiding. "The experience had destroyed whatever initiative I possessed," wrote Napoleon. "I felt myself in the clutches of some depressing influences which seemed like a nightmare. I was alive. I could move around. But I could not think of a single move by which I might continue to seek the goal which I had so long set for myself. I was rapidly becoming indifferent; worse still, I was becoming grouchy and irritable toward those who had given me shelter in my hour of need."

- But as usual, not overcome by adversity, Hill bounced back and again received backing for his 8-book series. The first volume,

*The Law of Success*, laid out 15 principles and represented what would be much of the thesis of his masterpiece, yet to come, *Think and Grow Rich*. The book took off, lightened the financial burden of Florence, and the wealth brought the family closer together. For an entire year the ride lasted. But then came the Stock Market Crash of 1929 and the beginning of the depression. By October, 1930, Florence was borrowing from her family again, and Napoleon had defaulted on a property.

- And then, the final aspects of the chain reaction that would give birth to the most influential book on personal success, inspiring entrepreneurs and leaders all over the world, began. In 1933, on the recommendation of Congressman Jennings Randolph, a long time supporter of Napoleon Hill's, the administration of President Franklin Delano Roosevelt hired Napoleon Hill as a speechwriter and public relations man for the National Recovery Administration. Napoleon Hill eventually requested a salary of $1 a year, and received what he asked for. But Florence and the children were not in as patriotic of a mood as he was. The sacrifice or foolishness – depending upon what perspective one takes – of Napoleon taking on such compensation and intense labor while his family languished in poverty was the final straw for Florence and, in 1935, she obtained an uncontested divorce when *Napoleon's own father*, James, paid for her to make the arrangements in the state of Florida because divorce was not legal in West Virginia. James and his son Napoleon hardly communicated with one another again. During this painful time, Napoleon worked even more intensely on his success philosophy. His biography describes, "Writing, lecturing and consulting to FDR kept Hill busy, but not busy enough. To cope with his post marital isolation, he found it necessary to work himself to exhaustion. Thus, to fill many long, lonely nights, he labored over several different manuscripts in preparation for the day Americans would once again dare to dream of success and to pursue it."

- Just as his money ran out, Napoleon remarried – to a woman named Rosa Lee. The couple had so little they had to move in with Napoleon's son, Blair, and his own new wife. The arrangement was a disaster – straining Napoleon's relationship with the son to whom he was closest. Their bond began to unravel under the pressure of Napoleon's criticism of his son, the close living quarters, and a loan made to Napoleon that was not repaid in a timely fashion. Blair and his wife divorced later, many believing this period doomed the marriage. The son that adored his father for helping him gain his hearing among other factors was now speaking of him like an enemy. In early 1938, Blair wrote his mother, Florence, a letter wherein he calls his dad an "unscrupulous, holier-than-thou, two-timing, double crossing good-for-nothing. Sometime I'm going to see that he pays and pays plenty for the way he treated you, treated me, treated David and Jimmy [Blair's brothers]!" Paradoxically, while Napoleon and Rosa Lee were living with Blair and his wife, the manuscript that would become *Think and Grow Rich!* was completed and re-written three times with Rosa Lee typing every page of every re-write.

Here, from *A Lifetime of Riches,* is the story of how the decision to publish the manuscript for *Think and Grow Rich* was made by publisher Mr. Andrew Pelton as well as its results:

After weeks of sleepless toil, Hill invited Andrew Pelton to the apartment and presented the manuscript to him. The publisher read the table of contents and thumbed through a few pages of text, then gave the eager Hills his verdict: It was just another self-help book, essentially the same as Hill's previous work and several other titles that he had published in recent years and which were not selling.

Despite the torture the Hills had endured to produce the manuscript, they received the publisher's sentiments with surprising aplomb. "We knew before he ever saw the manuscript that he was going to publish it," explained Hill. "We gave that matter no concern whatsoever…..

"After he had talked all afternoon analyzing the book and trying to prove to us it was not very different from other books…my wife suggested that he take the manuscript home with him, read it, and then he would know what was in it that was not in my previous books or in any other book he had published."

Rosa Lee was nothing if not persuasive with men, and Pelton assented. Three days later he appeared at their apartment once more, ready to take a chance on the book on one condition – that the title be changed to something more catchy.

In the lore surrounding this particular publishing venture, one story suggested that right up to the eve of the first printing the publisher wanted to call it *Use Your Noodle to Win More Boodle*. In the end, however, the book was published under the title *Think and Grow Rich!*, and its fame and popularity would begin immediately and last the rest of the century.

Andrew Pelton had every right to be reluctant to invest in an inspirational self-help book that spoke of riches and success in 1937 America. Although the New Deal had succeeded in getting the economy moving forward again, the pace of improvement was agonizingly slow. Millions of Americans were still out of work and millions more were underemployed. America's Great Depression was showing only the slightest glimmerings of dissipating; it would, in fact, extend through the remainder of the decade. There was no tangible reason to believe that Napoleon's new title would have any more appeal to a tattered and besieged nation than *The Magic Ladder to Success* created in the early thirties.

Playing his own gut hunch, Pelton not only printed *Think and Grow Rich*, he also slapped a $2.50 retail price on it and ordered five thousand copies in the first pressrun – a fairly optimistic quantity for the day.

Incredibly, that seemingly risky print order turned out to be woefully inadequate for the demand. Three weeks after the book went into distribution, the entire print run was sold out. There followed an endless succession of printings and larger print orders as the book became a huge best-seller. If anyone in America was looking for a tangible sign that private citizens were shaking off the mental and emotional stigma of the depression, *Think and Grow Rich!* provided it in hard sales figures. Shortly after its initial appearance, one insurance company purchased five thousand copies of the book in a single order. Tens of thousands more were purchased in other bulk orders, while hundreds of thousands of single-copy sales were being rung up in direct mail and retail store offerings.

Well over a million copies of the book were sold even before the depression lifted, and it would continue to sell in large volume for decades and generations to come – all over America and throughout the world. Ten years later, *Think and Grow Rich!* ranked fourth in a leading magazine's poll on books that most influenced the lives of the successful men of the forties. Fifty years later, the twenty-millionth copy of the book was sold; it remained an active title in thousands of libraries and was still stocked by leading bookstores throughout the country.

Why would a book once thought to be like any other succeed on such a grand scale?

The answer probably stems from the fact that the content of *Think and Grow Rich!* originated from Law of Success and Hill's uniquely Carnegie-inspired twenty-year investigation of what makes people succeed. The research itself, and the content of Law of Success, are among the most original works in modern American publishing.

Although Napoleon Hill obtained and learned much from the captains of business and industry that he studied – as well as from everyday entrepreneurs – of all of the themes that seem to dominate his legendary book, *Think and Grow Rich*, the idea that never disappears completely from view was given to him in an exchange with Andrew Carnegie, in their very first meeting:

**Napoleon Hill**: But what happens when a man knows what he wants, has a plan, puts it into action and meets with failure? Doesn't that destroy his confidence?

**Andrew Carnegie**: I hoped you would ask that because it is important to understand what I'm about to tell you. I believe that every failure carries within it – in the circumstances of the failure itself – the seed of an equivalent advantage. If you examine the lives of truly great leaders, you will discover that their success is in exact proportion to their mastery of failures. Life has a way of developing strength and wisdom in individuals through temporary defeat.

**Napoleon Hill:** Most people aren't going to believe that every failure has an equivalent advantage when they are overcome with the adversity. What does one do if the experience destroys one's self-confidence?

**Andrew Carnegie:** The best way to guard against being overwhelmed by failure is to discipline the mind to meet failure before it arrives.

Failure, adversity, perseverance, patience, persistence, endurance and faith are all words that one will find in the life struggle of the entrepreneur. One can clearly see this at work in the life of Napoleon Hill and the subjects featured in his classic book. The ability to overcome resistance and manage pain seems to be an unavoidable aspect of those who set goals and seek them. The word and concept that best embodies all of these factors and can be applied most broadly across human disciplines is *suffering*.

But how do we 'teach' young people what suffering is, much less how to handle it?

My experience in education has shown me that the problem is not so much 'teaching' it but rather being willing to incorporate what students already know about suffering. In other words, everybody 'learns' about disappointment, frustration, temporary defeat, failure, adversity, struggle and difficulty in their everyday life.

In that sense the course is not taught in a room, but rather, an entire world.

What a young person goes through at home, in the neighborhood, and in their school experience involves suffering.

What schools have had a tendency to do is advise students on how to manage the emotions they experience and certain skills and attitudes that prepare them to accept suffering as part of life.

However, what schools have *not* done is illustrate that suffering can, in fact, be a redemptive, energizing, enlightening, and above all, motivational experience which propels people to think harder and try new things which lead to new ideas, products, and services; yes, successful businesses.

In that sense, entrepreneurship and inventiveness cannot be taught as a curriculum but students can be shown how to observe how suffering played a role in the lives of great scientists, performers, and business leaders. Here, a study of the biographies and defining moments in the lives of such persons *is* the textbook.

What better person to start this with than a study of the painfully creative life of the author with the greatest impact on entrepreneurship – Napoleon Hill.

# Chapter 11: Two Skills a Student Must Get From College

"No student knows his subject: the most he knows is where and how to find out the things he does not know."
### - Woodrow T. Wilson (28th President of the United States)

"Take the attitude of a student, never be too big to ask questions, never know too much to learn something new."

### - Og Mandino

In this era of social media and mobile phones where individuals share more but often in a briefer and more abbreviated manner – while enjoying the advantages of this myself – I've also noticed a challenge, and perhaps a problem.

It feels like we are learning more about many things but at the same time not necessarily doing more with the increase. In some ways education itself is changing with the advances in technology and convenience. Many things have been made more efficient but the benefits have not automatically resulted in greater academic performance.

I'm not one of those persons who thinks that the increased use of calculators in math and science class and search engines in history and social studies influences students to become lazy, but I do believe that the attention span, discipline and skill set that is required for projects that require in-depth research from a variety of sources (not necessarily available online) is lacking at times.

The computer and Internet has taken the place of the library without bringing all of what the library has to offer online.

As a result, bits and pieces of information have become more common than original sources of information in their unedited form.

This, in my opinion, makes it much more difficult for educators to teach concepts and lessons that require more time, effort, and patience.

In short, data and information have taken the place of knowledge, understanding and wisdom – the latter three areas of which are essential to the fulfillment of the second part of our definition of an entrepreneur (one who conceives or perceives an opportunity *and builds an organization to pursue it*).

One can conceive and perceive a business opportunity or an idea, and even plan one, relying primarily on data and information, but no business can be built without the more in-depth and broader areas of knowledge, understanding and wisdom.

This crystallized in my mind when I first learned of a book that was the final report of a group of senior Canadian government officials, private-sector executives, and researchers working together between 1990 and 1997.

The primary focus of this group – the Roundtable on Governing in an Information Society – was to explore and develop more effective ways of governing in this rapidly changing world.

In *Renewing Governance: Governing by Learning in the Information Age* by Steven A. Rosell we read:

We are exploring a territory for which there is no reliable map. The inadequacy of our conceptual apparatus to make sense of proliferating and unfamiliar information is usually described and experienced as 'information overload'. But it may be more accurate (and useful) to see the real problem as the insufficient capacity of our existing frameworks and methods of interpretation – our existing mental maps – to translate that data and information into meaningful knowledge. This formulation is based in part on a distinction suggested by Harlan Cleveland:

- data are unrefined ore, undifferentiated facts without contexts;

- information is refined ore, organized data, but data that we have not yet internalized (the newspapers we have not yet read, the course we have not yet taken);

- knowledge is information that we have internalized (integrated with our own internal frameworks.)

These distinctions became important parts of the vocabulary of the project, helping us to see that the process of translating data and information into knowledge (the process by which data and information are interpreted, given meaning, and so made useful as a basis for action) is central to effective governance.

Although not perfectly how I would describe knowledge, the above is helpful in making a point about a difference between information and knowledge, particularly in this age of talk radio, Internet news, the 24-hour cable news and opinion cycle. Information is more of an external or superficial phenomenon, while knowledge involves the internalization of information with an awareness of its factual nature. Understanding revolves around the *meaning* of knowledge, and wisdom is the application of what you understand.

Again, this generally describes our learning which revolves around conversation, observation, reading, meditation and experience (which always involves suffering).

One of the factors that all of us, especially children in school, must be careful of is the degree to which we increasingly rely upon exposure to information sources as our primary means of learning.

Many of our young people have not been shown how to discern and make the distinction between data, information, knowledge, understanding, and wisdom.

That is why whenever I get a chance to speak with high school students entering colleges and universities, I stress the importance of them not only performing well academically, but also focusing on two areas of the higher education experience which they will most likely not ever again be in such a great position to master: conducting research in libraries and networking with their peers.

University libraries are an excellent way to learn how data, information, knowledge, and understanding are organized and categorized. Understanding how this is done and made available to people – regardless to their background – can be very instructive to someone looking to start a business and serve a wide customer base. Every library, by nature of its function and service, represents a universe of how to conceive and perceive ideas and opportunities and how to build an organization.

A prospective entrepreneur who does not take the time to get acquainted with how libraries organize information is losing a great opportunity to pick up keys on how to build a business organization. Although most may not think of it this way at first, a librarian may be an entrepreneur's best friend.

One of the best libraries that one can consider – free of charge – as an example in this regard is the Library of Congress (LOC) in Washington, D.C., which has a total of 144,562,233 items in the collections, including (according to information on its website):

- 21,814,555 cataloged books in the Library of Congress classification system
- 11,701,147 books in large type and raised characters, incunabula (books printed before 1501), monographs and serials, bound newspapers, pamphlets, technical reports, and other printed material

- 111,046,531 items in the nonclassified (special) collections. These include:
  - o 3,052,857 audio materials, such as discs, tapes, talking books, and other recorded formats
  - o 63,718,170 total manuscripts
  - o 5,391,200 maps
  - o 16,206,259 microforms
  - o 6,001,971 pieces of sheet music
  - o 14,426,474 visual materials, including:
    - ▪ 1,213,180 moving images
    - ▪ 12,5557,200 photographs
    - ▪ 101,449 posters
    - ▪ 554,645 prints and drawings

The LOC also says it:

- Circulated nearly 24 million disc, cassette and Braille items to more than 800,000 blind and physically handicapped patrons.
- Registered 382,086 claims to copyright.
- Prepared 1,491 legal research reports for Congress and other federal agencies through the Law Library.
- Recorded more than 81 million visits and 630 million page-views on the Library's website. At year's end, the Library's online primary source files totaled 19 million.

What a wealth of relevant experience for any person interested in starting a business. On a smaller scale, free public libraries represent this same value.

Every student, if nothing else, should gain mastery of how to research a college or university library.

The other important objective I see in the college experience is the chance to benefit from a unique networking experience that will serve students for the rest of their lives, and their business prospects.

I started thinking about this in a new way after learning some things about the relationship between individuals who have had a close-knit military experience and how that has had a positive impact on their entrepreneurial future.

Describing how this plays out in Israel and then relating it to college and high school experience of students in the U.S., economist Reuven Brenner writes (bold emphasis is mine):

A second major contribution to the Israeli …success story is the draft. Three-year army service is obligatory for Israeli men; and if they choose to study engineering or other specialties before enlisting, they must serve for five years. **This ends up providing many people with the chance to develop discipline and perseverance, and in many cases, even find the team they want to start a business with. People get answers to questions such as: Who has leadership qualities? Managerial ones? Technical ones? Who can work well with others and under stress? In the U.S. most future business careers start with undergraduate studies or an MBA program (where people hope to meet other smart, ambitious youngsters) and participation in team sports (a way of discovering personal traits).**

This shows that the people we meet in college tend to not only be a significant portion of our friends later in life but also a great field for us to find qualified partners in business. This is because we get to see individuals in a more private and social light and in settings and circumstances which reveal their talents, skills, and character – the qualities that reveal the nine Personalities that business revolves around.

Whether in a dormitory, sorority, fraternity, sports team, dining hall, rally, student center, or campus bus, we are in a position to learn something that helps us get to know people through observation, conversation or experience.

Unfortunately, students are not told this *before* they arrive on campus and are unprepared to have their eye trained on this sort of thing.

That's why they need a good mentor in their lives.

# Chapter 12: The Importance of a Mentor

"Be the change you want to see in the world."

**- Gandhi**

"Mentoring is a brain to pick, an ear to listen, and a push in the right direction."

**- John Crosby**

If there is a theme in this book that is consistent, it is that, as of right now, instruction in creativity and entrepreneurial development are not consistently featured aspects or even priorities within much of the elementary and secondary school system of the United States of America.

This reality means that anyone sincerely committed to these areas of education will have to introduce them in a system and culture that has been resistant, negligent, or largely unaware of them, or will have to build alternative institutions where these subjects can be taught openly and in a supportive environment.

In developing educational courses and guiding schools which place an emphasis on business instruction, I have been blessed to provide students in high school with a curriculum focused on entrepreneurship, small business, and venture capital.

Yet and still, I realize that students need more outside of what takes place in school to support what they receive in these areas.

This brings me to the critical role that mentors can serve.

When I speak of business mentors I am not just speaking of persons who have a wealth of knowledge and experience who are willing to spend time with students in conversation and quality time together. I am speaking of individuals with business experience who are intimately aware of the course material that the student is learning about and who can reinforce it. In that sense I see business mentors for students being most effective when they are connected not just to the individual student but to the class.

One of the most powerful experiences that I've had was a time when I invited a guest lecturer into a class to support a discussion we were having based upon his thoughts in reaction to an article on entrepreneurship.

The article was published in *Black Enterprise* magazine, written by Renita Burns, and titled, "Natural Born Hustler: Is Entrepreneurship Learned or Innate?" It is a question, subject and debate that many scholars, journalists, and businesspersons have contemplated and discussed for years.

The main argument made in the article by Renita Burns was:

Are entrepreneurs born or made?

My argument: The odds of becoming an entrepreneur are based on a combination of natural talent and learned skill. Successful entrepreneurs are innately creative and innovative people with unparalleled ambition. But the basics of marketing, sales, and bookkeeping are learned.

While I do believe there is likely a high correlation between those who were raised around entrepreneurs and those who become entrepreneurs, how one was raised is not the sole determining factor. Furthermore, becoming a successful entrepreneur isn't exclusively dependent upon whether mom and dad are their own bosses, but more so on being able to execute, recognize business opportunities, and take risks.

The idea is akin to that of child prodigies—musicians, math whizzes, etc. The talent is there and the children, for some reason, gravitate to an instrument or field of knowledge. But that skill must also be nurtured by someone who can teach the child the fundamentals of the craft. In the area of entrepreneurship, a great example is Black Enterprise 2009 Teenpreneur Award winner Jordan Culpepper, the 13-year-old founder and CEO of Buttons By Jordan. The teen's precocious entrepreneurial instinct was nurtured and supported by family and friends.

A study by Scott A. Shane, professor of entrepreneurial studies at the Weatherhead School of Management at Case Western University in Cleveland and author of The Illusions of Entrepreneurship, found that the tendency to be an entrepreneur is heritable—or able to be explained by genetic factors. In a blog written for the New York Times last month, Shane said, "The tendency to identify business opportunities and the tendency to start new businesses have a common genetic source. This pattern suggests that genetic factors might influence the odds of people becoming entrepreneurs by affecting their ability to identify new business opportunities."

Our guest lecturer, Ric, had publicly written some of the following in response:

I read your article, "Natural Born Hustler: Is Entrepreneurship Learned or Innate?" dated October 26, 2009 with great interest

…You make some excellent points that open the door to an important dialogue that touch on or cross barriers, transcending dimensions like race, gender, and age. In some respects entrepreneurship is a universal phenomenon and in others it is shaped by the parameters of identity. But as it relates to your interesting article, there are a few concepts that I'd like to bring to the table of discussion – namely the bearing that suffering, kinship systems, and the ability to access knowledge and transfer it across generations has on your subject. This goes well beyond the factors of genetics, family, mentoring and modeling upon which you focus.

First, I define an entrepreneur as one who perceives or conceives of an opportunity and builds an organization to pursue it.

I do believe that perception and conception, although they can be sharpened by certain exercises and states of mind, are significantly innate or biologically determined. And I also believe that most of what is involved in building a business organization is learned or has to be transferred through teaching or training.

As you note, "Successful entrepreneurs are innately creative and innovative people with unparalleled ambition. But the basics of marketing, sales, and bookkeeping are learned."

However, I think the subject that few economists and journalists deal with is the impact that suffering or the experience of a loss or shock has on the critical factor of *making the decision* to become an entrepreneur. What I am suggesting is that entrepreneurs are neither 'born' genetically, nor produced by education as much as they are created by circumstance.

…Suffering leads to risk-taking because it causes us to think harder. This is where I caution people to be careful about making genetic determinism arguments ('I'm born this way.') without placing the proper emphasis on how environment combines with our anatomy and physiology to shape us.

You quote author Scott A. Shane as writing "The tendency to identify business opportunities and the tendency to start new businesses have a common genetic source. This pattern suggests that genetic factors might influence the odds of people becoming entrepreneurs by affecting their ability to identify new business opportunities."

This is true but biological determinism does not always explain the process and context that undergirds or activates certain behavior and the decisions we make and why. For example, I've noted how the 'shocks' and disrupting events in our lives can disorient and confuse us, but also lead to a biological state of arousal that allows us to tap into greater thinking power.

In addition, I have yet to see any scientist explain how genetic factors affect how sudden and powerful insights – epiphanies – come to us. Epiphanies are the sudden perception of something – including opportunities – and they can occur when we are in very relaxed or intense states of mind.

And I haven't even begun to get into the power of the subconscious mind and what affirmation, visualization and prayer enable us to do.

I personally saw a lot of value in both points of view and thought it would be good for the 11th grade class to discuss it. So I shared my thoughts with one of the course instructors, Mr. Dawkins, who liked the idea and facilitated a week's worth of classroom discussion around it.

Initially I was concerned that some of the language and points made in both articles would be a bit too technical or complicated for the students to handle but any such fears were shown to be unmerited by the moments of enthusiastic response displayed by the students over the course of the week.

Although I still had my reservations, after a few days of class conversation and consulting with Mr. Dawkins, we invited Ric to sit in on a class and offer his thoughts as a guest expert and lecturer.

What took place was remarkable, the students in several circles had a cordial, spirited, and highly intelligent debate, that was so sophisticated that Ric himself, who had prepared remarks, felt no need to add to anything that had been shared in conversation other than to encourage the students to continue certain lines of dialogue with one another.

He became more interviewer than lecturer and the students were unusually poised in his presence.

It was the first time I ever saw a guest lecturer 'cancel' his own lecture in person – so humorous and edifying at the same time.

At the end of the class, Ric personally exchanged his business cards with the students and remained in e-mail and even phone contact with them some throughout the year.

He became a remote or long-distance mentor, but perhaps, in my opinion, with a more positive influence than if he were in town on a daily basis talking to the students one-on-one over a meal.

The feedback received directly from the students the very next class after he left, showed me we really were on to something with our hybrid guest lecture-mentor format and that there is something missing in traditional classroom instruction that was missing and which had never produced anything like I was seeing.

Below is an unedited summary of the student reaction to the entire experience:

**Guiding Question/Focus:** What made Friday's conversation so powerful? Think about it in terms of what were the factors that led to the high engagement, respect, and personal connections? Write specifically about the impact the Guest, the Structure of the Class, having 2 articles to discuss and the Personal Connection ability had on the Power.

**Purpose:** We want to analyze these factors in order to create more experiences that reflect the high level of engagement that we witnessed on Friday.

| Guest: | Structure of Class: |
|---|---|
| • He was great & treated us like adults<br>• He didn't just talk to us—I hate being talked to like I don't know or I'm a child—he talked to us on "our" level<br>• Though neither Ms. Desai nor Ric didn't get to argue, they were very respectful towards the students and seemed very excited to be there. I liked hearing from him and got some good pointers<br>• Listened more than talked. Included everyone in the conversation. Made the conversation comfortable<br>• Ric was so cool, calm, collective, and understanding<br>• He made everyone feel they were "equals" since he sat in the circle rather than be a "guest speaker"—he was just a guest<br>• He was a powerful guest because he listened to us | • Was powerful to have it in a circle because everyone felt more comfortable to share<br>• Being able to talk without the teacher interfering<br>• Having the spontaneity to just express what I think of at any given time is amazing<br>• Everyone who wanted to participate, participated, stated their argument, and backed it up. They all listened to one another<br>• Everyone was involved in one way or another. People were respectful<br>• Warm, respective, constructive, positive<br>• It was nice to have the respect of this structure because all the rest of the day things are being 'told' to us and 'done to us'—this was different<br>• Was powerful because everyone was being respectful to the person speaking |

- Being in the presence of one who has studied entrepreneurship professionally is very powerful, being around Ric's energy, he had so much experience, knowledge, and entrepreneurial embodiment
- He was interested, proud, he was HERE, he voiced his own opinion, and he remembered which comment came from who
- It was powerful to have one of the authors that wrote one of the articles there to tell us his thoughts on the discussion
- It was powerful to have him there because everything we talked about we looked back at him and he would tell us if we were on the same page
- He was very powerful in the information with the response to the first article
- The class was very excited that we had someone here from DC!
- His presence was inspiring—it made everyone want to impress!
- The power of the conversation didn't come from him, it came from him being there
- Ric was powerful because he wrote articles and a book on the topic we were talking about
- It made the conversation real serious having Ric there. It made it feel like it was on a very mature level
- Having Ric here was very powerful all on its own. Ric is a

- The Socratic seminar structure of those who were debating, choosing to be in on the conversation, was powerful. It allowed for those who were really eager to speak, to choose to speak. It also allowed a variety of opinion that had strong beliefs put into it
- It was good to have an inner and outer circle. Nobody talked over each other
- The way we were in a circle was powerful because everyone had something insightful to say and everyone showed respect to whomever was speaking
- The structure was very strong because the conversation would stay in the circle
- The structure of the class was not just powerful but well done. I was able to sit in the outer circle and take good notes and listen to a great conversation that was happening inside the circle
- The structure was powerful because we had students having a class discussion that flowed steady and other students recording the discussion
- I think it helped everyone stay focused and everybody had something to do
- Respectfulness, everyone was doing something, everyone could see each other

| | |
|---|---|
| very smart man and he gave key insight to a deeper understandings of the topic.<br>• It gave us a chance to ask him personally about what he wrote<br>• He seems like a great entrepreneur who knows how to achieve in life<br>• He was very friendly and it was a joy to have him share his opinion with his<br>• He was very respectful and treated us like equals | |
| **Had 2 articles as a resource:**<br><br>• I don't think it was so much about the articles, it was about us and our opinions<br>• The articles somewhat helped but all they did for me was give me a bit of info here and there<br>• Very good points were made from both sides. Some students in the circle shared their own personal connections to the articles and I thought that was a strong experience to back up their arguments<br>• A lot of information<br>• Powerful because you could use them as references<br>• The amount of information on the subject<br>• The articles were powerful because we could make a connection to our own lives<br>• Both articles supported the | **Personal Connections:**<br><br>• The debates were specific, detailed, and deep. A couple people shared based on their own experience, and others used an actual person to support the debate. Everyone just really got into it<br>• I thought the debate went pretty well. I agree, it was powerful. Students got to share their thoughts on the articles and they respected one another when they disagreed. I heard some very good arguments from both sides and some of them I could relate to, mostly the ones related to determination<br>• Hearing other stories was powerful<br>• Sharing my personal entrepreneur experience from being an entrepreneur was powerful<br>• It was powerful to talk about my life being in the system, how I've raised myself, how my situation makes me or breaks me<br>• I think the conversation last Friday |

- question
- I really liked how one person can just think about his/her life and write books about it!
- It was a big help to the conversation
- The two articles were good because we had two sides of the story, not just one
- Helped to have so much info about the topic
- It was good to have articles so we could see from both sides of the fence
- It really helped because I think it made the conversation deep and think harder. It lasted longer because people had more to say
- The two articles helped us form our opinions
- Provided evidence to support both sides of the argument

- set the tone for future guest speakers in this class
- I really liked having him here. It was fun and cool
- It was easier to bring it back to the reality level instead of just surface…the personal connections made it so much deeper
- The environment was so respectful that people were comfortable to share
- I liked how comfortable they were and shared their personal stories
- Provided us with the examples and helped us understand the topic and each other better

## Other Comments:

- We should do this again!
- I wasn't here when Ric came but I would have liked to have been here and hear the discussions and debates. He sounded like a smart individual and I could've learned some valuable information
- My parents being quiet, like me, I can see that some things are passed on and influenced by parents. I'm quiet. I don't want to be. Participating in class proves that most things are nurtured on your own
- I think the guest made me feel like everyone's opinion was important
- Last Friday was the best day I have had in a long time! The convo was so deep!!! Everybody's comments made the conversation more interesting because everybody's opinions made pretty good sense!
- I felt the class on Friday was a good discussion because we all got into the conversation deeply and said what we wanted to say about being born or being made entrepreneurs. I really liked that we all agreed in a way but not really

- It was powerful because I learned so much from my classmates and to see people going back and forth changed my thoughts about the whole entrepreneurship thing
- I think it was a powerful conversation of Friday because there was a good conversation going on. They had powerful statements, agreements, and opinions. They knew what they were talking about and had a very interesting topic to discuss
- It was powerful because everybody put in their own thought and participated
- Even though I wasn't in the inside circle, I think the conversation was powerful. There was a lot of different opinions shared and each one had a good point
- I thought it was pretty powerful because we had many people defending many points of view and Ric had joined us in person
- I did find it powerful because it gave us students the power to direct our own conversation and prove our points

<<<<>>>>

From the reaction that Mr. Dawkins received it was clear that there were several factors contributing to such an overwhelmingly positive experience, as expressed by the students.

First, the course syllabus or reading material – the two articles – were not formal in the sense of a textbook and did not disqualify opinions from legitimate debate. Second, the students were positioned at the center of the class by a teacher who cared and an outsider whom they believed to be an expert – making them secure in articulating their viewpoints to one another. Third, the subject matter was supplementary to the 'official' curriculum and therefore less pressure was present or associated with mastering it in order to pass a test or receive a positive homework grade. And fourth, the guest was coming to affirm the content and direction of the class and not distract from it with an unfamiliar or unnecessary contribution.

These four elements embody the next level to which I believe mentorship can evolve.

A more intense and potentially transformative experience takes place when both the student and potential mentor are both interested *in* and motivated *by* the school subject and allowed to interact and form a relationship around it in both formal and informal ways.

By utilizing the classroom and subject matter as the place to begin a meaningful relationship, schools can play a unique role in facilitating a mutually rewarding and beneficial relationship that has the potential for both a lifelong impact and continued reinforcement of school subject matter.

By connecting a student's growing awareness of themselves with entrepreneurship and mentoring in a classroom setting, benefits that no test can measure can be generated.

# Epilogue

"In 1900, in his book *Corporations and the Public Welfare*, James Dill warned that the most critical social question of the day was figuring out how to get rid of the small entrepreneur, yet at the same time retain his loyalty 'to a system based on private enterprise.' The small entrepreneur had been the heart of the American republican ideal, the soul of its democratic strength. So the many school training habits which led directly to small entrepreneurship had to be eliminated."

**- The Underground History of American Education A Schoolteacher's Intimate Investigation Into The Prison of Modern Schooling by John Taylor Gatto; published by: The Oxford Village Press, Oxford, New York, 2006.**

"There is nothing more threatening to an established order – any order than opening up, deepening, democratizing capital markets – accountably, allowing people to leverage their inventive, enterprising spirit. True, this would also disperse power – political power in particular. The deeper capital markets would also threaten established industries and commerce. Entrepreneurs, brilliant and ambitious as they might be, are *not* a threat…But entrepreneurs with access to *different, independent* sources of risk capital – now that's threatening…"

**- Reuven Brenner's book review of The Invention of Enterprise: Entrepreneurship from Ancient Mesopotamia to Modern Times**

The future of education is in a place we – as professional educators – have rarely journeyed to, or explored.

That 'place' is not some far off land, emerging technology, or cutting edge seminar critiquing the profession.

No, it is the heart, mind and soul of students themselves.

*Ami Desai*

Their passions, talents, and interests are an untapped oasis, goldmine, and territory more in harmony with the root meaning of education (*educo*, 'to draw out that which is within,' as it has been defined), than our 'rules of instruction', curricula, and lesson plans.

This book has placed emphasis on a particular field of development and study – entrepreneurship – which may, more than any other, reveal this fact.

At a time when young people are ready, willing, and able to handle business education and creative risk-taking, it is a shame that we simply don't give them that chance.

My focus has particularly been on those of high school and early college years because it is simply more obvious that, by then, the basics (and beyond) of economic activity can be grasped and taught. And yes, at that early age our youth can even be 'trained' or 'apprenticed' into application of the science and art of business.

Luke Johns described this state of readiness in our young people brilliantly in a December 22, 2010 article in the *Financial Times*, "Go Forth, Young Business Founder", an installment in his regular 'The Entrepreneur column. He writes:

I get the impression that twentysomethings believe in freedom and independence. Spending your time building your own company is a pretty effective way of achieving those goals. And in some respects grabbing that opportunity as young as you can is a great idea. The sooner you get used to the glories and miseries of self-employment, the better. Most important, you have so little to lose: no dependants, minimal outgoings, and all the time in the world. It is the best phase in your adult life to experiment and perhaps fail. At 21 you are young enough to try again, learn from experience and do it better next time. When you are young you have boundless energy and less inhibition about radical suggestions.

The hope and ambition of someone entering the world of work at the start of their adult life should be boundless. Who else can believe in the impossible?

The older generation has wisdom, but it can also be cynical and too proud, too comfortable – and, perhaps, too pessimistic. On the other hand, someone fresh can have a different vision, an idea of a better world.

Yet, we neglect watering this 'different vision' or feeding 'an idea of a better world', for the thirteen most important years of a person's life.

That's the *secret* staring us right in the face.

By starting from within and working our way out of a universe in miniature form – a beautiful human being – and _not_ the premise that certain forms of learning are irrelevant or unattainable for a young mind, we truly can be involved in a learning and development process, which waits on no classroom to begin, or finish.

My experience as a mentor, educator, and administrator has not just provided evidence, but proven to me that when young people are allowed to study and learn from themselves, teach one another, and connect with caring persons, inside and outside of a classroom setting, a certain form of energy is tapped into and can be converted or translated into a transformative experience resulting in effective culture and discipline, increased self-confidence, and heightened academic performance.

Any form of education that teaches young people *away* from themselves – their passions, interests, and talents – is *mis*education, and there is plenty of anecdotal evidence in society to back this up – drop-out and incarceration levels and unemployment rates are some of the best leading indicators in that regard, not to mention the disinterest and boredom which greets too many sincere educators working in classrooms each day.

Even if the goal of school is to 'get a job', or 'good education', there are just too many metrics which indicate that even this clear standard is not being met at the level that has been advertised.

So, something *must* be done and something *can* be done.

Increased emphasis on creativity. Increased emphasis on entrepreneurship. Increased emphasis on mentorship (tied to classroom curriculum).

There is simply no reason for this to be a secret any longer.

# Selected Bibliography

## Books

Bossidy, Larry and Charan, Ram. *Execution: The Discipline of Getting Things Done.* New York: Crown Business, 2002

Bureau of Labor Statistics, U.S. Department of Labor, *Occupational Outlook Handbook*, 2010-11 Edition, Bulletin 2800. Superintendent of Documents, U.S. Government Printing Office, Washington, DC, 2006

Evanson, David R. *Where To Go When The Bank Says No.* New York: Bloomberg Press, 1998

Frankyl, Viktor E. Man's *Search For Meaning.* Boston: Beacon Press, 2006

Frankyl, Viktor E. *The Will To Meaning: Foundations and Applications of Logotherapy.* New York: Plum Publishing, 1998

George, Jr., Claude S. The *History of Management Thought.* Englewood Cliffs: Prentice-Hall, 1968

Gerber, Michael E. *The E-Myth Revisited.* New York: Harper-Collins, 1995

Hill, Napoleon. *Think And Grow Rich.* New York: Ballantine Books, 1987

Holyoak, Keith J. and Morrison, Robert G. *The Cambridge Handbook of Thinking and Reasoning. Cambridge, United Kingdom: Cambridge University Press, 2005*

Haddock, Frank, Channing. *The Power of Will.* Whitefish: Kessinger Publishing, 2007

Landers, Kirk and Ritt, Jr., Michael J. *A Lifetime of Riches: The Biography of Napoleon Hill.* New York: Penguin Books, 1995

Muhammad, Cedric. *The Entrepreneurial Secret.* Washington D.C.: CM Cap Publishing 2009

Rosell, Steven A. *Renewing Governance: Governing By Learning In The Information Age.* Ontario and New York: Oxford Publishing, 1999

Ruggiero, Vincent Ryan. *Becoming A Critical Thinker.* Stamford: Wadsorth Publishing, 2005

## Articles

Advani, Asheesh. "How To Value Your Startup." *Entrepreneur* (September 7, 2004).

Burns, Renita. "Natural Born Hustler: Is Entrepreneurship Learned or Innate?". Black Enterprise (October 26, 2009)

Giwerc, David. "The AD/HD Entrepreneur." *About.com* (2003). (http://entrepreneurs.about.com/library/weekly/uc011103a.htm)

Sanchez, Lorenzo. "School Reformers: If You Want To Help, Listen To Youth." *Education news Colorado eNewsletter* (October 14, 2008).

Chivvis, Dana. "A Lancaster, Pa., high school is under fire for implementing a new program that has created separate homerooms for black juniors." *AOLnews.com* (January 28, 2011).

Heathfield, Susan. "Dress for Work Success: A Business Casual Dress Code." *About.com.* (http://humanresources.about.com/od/workrelationships/a/dress_code .htm).

Mullins, John W. "Why Business Plans Don't Deliver." *Wall Street Journal* (June 22, 2009).

## Public Studies

Chapman, C., Laird, J., and Kewal Ramani, A. (2008), Trends in High School Dropout and Completion Rates in the United States: 1972–2008. Washington D.C.: National Center For Education Statistics U.S. Department of Education, Institute of Education Sciences

## Transcripts

Proctor, Shonika. (November 9, 2009). "Commentary- Exposing Hidden leaders" *Nightly Business Report* [TV broadcast]. Miami, Florida: Public Broadcasting Service (http://www.pbs.org/nbr/site/onair/transcripts/nbr_transcripts_091109/)

www.ingramcontent.com/pod-product-compliance
Lightning Source LLC
LaVergne TN
LVHW011230080426
835509LV00005B/427